Scandinavian Cooking
made easy

Savory dishes from the four northern sisters: Denmark, Finland, Norway, Sweden

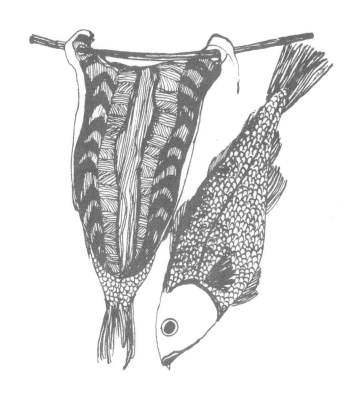

Galahad Books • New York City

Scandinavian Cooking made easy published by Galahad Books, New York City

This edition published by arrangement with 'Round the World Books Inc., New York, New York

Additional Picture Contributions:
• pg. 36, pg. 38; Atalanta Corp. (Finland Cheese Importers) •
• pg. 54, pg. 83; DAK FOODS, INC., East Brunswick, N.J. and DAK Meat Packers Ltd., Roskilde, Denmark •
• pg. 7, pg. 9; Denmark Cheese Association, Toronto, Canada •
• pg. 22, pg. 25; Dofo Cheese A.M.B.A., Denmark •
• pg. 49 top; Ideal Flatbread •
• pg. 85; Peter F. Heering •
• pg. 18; Tuborg Breweries, Baltimore, Maryland •

Additional Recipe Contributions:
• Finntastic soup, pg. 36, Dilled peas Helsinki, pg 38; Atalanta Corp. (Finland Cheese Importers) •
• Smørrebrød, pg. 23, Danish pea soup, pg. 34, Creamed cauliflower, pg. 37, Danish mustard sauce, pg. 41, Danish fried chicken, pg. 51, Samsoe chicken, pg. 52, Danish meatballs, pg. 56, Danish loin of pork, pg. 58; Jørgen Berlin •
• Baked ham and eggs, pg. 54, Danish ham and potato dinner, pg. 54, Baked ham with mustard sauce, pg. 83; DAK FOODS, INC., East Brunswick, N.J. and DAK Meat Packers Ltd., Roskilde, Denmark •
• Danish Fondue, pg. 25; Dofo Cheese A.M.B.A., Denmark •
• Peter Heering delight, pg. 85; Peter F. Heering •

Series designed by Margaret Verner

Library of Congress Catalog Card Number: 79-52184

ISBN: 0-88365-415-6

Printed in the United States of America

Contents

Scandinavia at the table

INTRODUCTION

Denmark, Norway, Sweden and Finland, the four most northerly countries of Europe, are usually pronounced together in one single breath as "Scandinavia" But although they do all have very much in common, they are in fact four quite independent countries, three of which are proud monarchies. Earlier in the history of Scandinavia, a kaleidoscope of political combinations once existed: Sweden united with Norway and Denmark, Sweden with Finland, and Denmark with Norway. Thus each country has long had a great influence on the other three. But they have all still retained certain unique and unmistakable characteristics.

Scandinavians may appear a bit reserved and self-contained at first, but they share an extremely deep love of nature, of silence and solitude. They have a reputation as an easy-going, companionable and hospitable people whose door is always cordially open. Their spare time is usually engaged in outdoor sports; not team sports but recreation in which the individual is alone with nature: skiing on the silent, snow-covered mountain slopes, ice-skating over the cold surface of frozen lakes, canoeing, hiking, fishing and sailing. The long summer evenings in the land of the Midnight Sun are usually spent outdoors, but the long, dark and cold winter is spent around the warm and cosy open fireplace. (It is no coincidence that the housebound Scandinavians have set a standard of interior decoration and comfortable furniture design that is world renowned.) Getting together with friends to eat and drink the long winter evening away is elevated almost to a ritual in Scandinavia, and nowhere else is there so much imagination, skill and artistry applied to setting the candle laden table.

The real roots of Scandinavian eating lie in the climate. People were forced to stock supplies for the long winter, and in this way the process of preserving meat, fish, vegetables and fruit has been developed into a fine art. Nowhere else in the world can there be found so many different ways of drying, smoking and curing meat and fish. This is a very ancient art: the Vikings who sailed a thousand years ago to Iceland, Greenland and even North America, carried with them smoked meat and dried, salted fish for the long weeks at sea.

But in spite of all the resemblances the Scandinavian countries have to each other, there are still enormous differences, and anyone thoroughly familiar with one country cannot claim familiarity with any of the other three. Centuries of shared history have still left individual characteristics and traditions so different that each country is unique. This is true even in the

cooking and dining habits of the four countries. Perhaps this is best revealed in the old saying: "The Danes live to eat, the Norwegians eat to live, and the Swedes eat to drink". The Finns are not included so let us complete the saying by adding: ". . . and the Finns drink to eat".

The famous Danish Smørrebrød

8

DENMARK

Denmark is Scandinavia's Promised Land, overflowing with milk and honey. Nowhere is the grass greener and thicker and nowhere do the cows give whiter and richer milk and sweeter cream. The vegetable gardens (first planted in the sixteenth century by Dutch, who migrated to Denmark but grew homesick for their familiar fresh green vegetables) produce fresh, tender, young vegetables early in the spring. The orchards yield delicious apples and ripe, sweet cherries (the source of a famous cherry liqueur). Pink, well-fed pigs grunt with satisfaction in this land of natural abundance. In the sea live small red, tasty shrimp and Baltic herring, and in the Limfjord grow large, pearl-colored oysters.

Festive eating and drinking are a sturdy tradition in Denmark and every visitor in Denmark is received in a generous and friendly fashion.

In Danish delicatessens the most inviting and appetizing foods are displayed in overflowing abundance: smoked salmon and eel, cheeses, sausages, ham and the most delicious varieties of fish and game. Eating and drinking are so much a national pastime, that it was not considered out of the ordinary when the late King Frederick appeared on his palace balcony to greet the people of Copenhagen, still wearing his napkin tucked around his neck.

The Danes begin their day with a breakfast of strong, tasty coffee and delicious sweet coffee rolls, so fine, light and crispy that they have no equal anywhere else in the world. Oddly enough, they call these "Wienerbrød", Viennese rolls, while we know them as the famed Danish pastry.

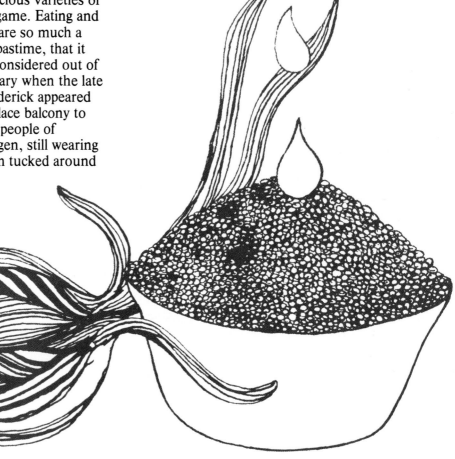

A selection of Danish cheeses

At about one o'clock, time for lunch, the Danes eat their famous "Smørrebrød". This literally means "bread spread with butter", but the butter is actually a minor ingredient, barely visible under the three or four layers of delicious garnishes that cover the bread. They make a colorful pattern that delights both the eye and the taste buds – thick slices of smoked fish or meat,

ham, hard-boiled or scrambled eggs, mayonnaise, potatoes, horseradish, fruit sauce or compôte, cold fish or shellfish, roasted meat, fresh vegetables. Almost anything can go into a Smørrebrød, so long as it is colorful in appearance and surprising in taste. One restaurant in Copenhagen has over 200 different varieties of Smørrebrød and they are all deliciously

described in a menu more than three feet long! These Smørrebrød are prepared to order and flown to many other countries in Western Europe.

In the evening, the Danes eat a hearty dinner, a roast with vegetables. The meal usually ends with one of the many sweet combinations of rich cream and fruit for which the Danes are famous.

The gently rolling Danish landscape, with its green and luscious pastures, is the home of Denmark's dairy herds, famed for their sweet white cream.

Past Copenhagen's famous spiral-steepled City Hall clatter the hoofs of drayhorses, pulling cartloads of foamy Danish lager beer.

And at the famous Tivoli amusement park in Copenhagen, colorful fireworks light up those very few hours between sunset and sunrise.

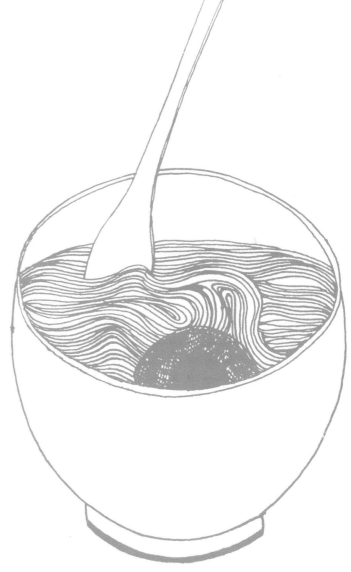

FINLAND

Finland is a mysterious country of deep solitude, of light, opal-colored summer nights and hard, cold, bitter and dark winters, and of 60,000 lakes that sparkle among somber, green forests of fir trees. Strictly speaking the Finns are not really Scandinavians. Their origins lie somewhere in the faraway steppes of Central Asia and their unpronounceable language is a reminder of their distant and misty past.

They are above all the people of the sauna. The sauna is the pivot around which Finnish life turns, and even the Finnish Cabinet has been known to meet in one. A sauna bath (in which you sit in a small, smotheringly hot room with pine-wood walls, where the temperature can rise anywhere from 225° to 250°, rubbing yourself with a stiff brush and soap and then going under a cold shower or for a swim in a cold lake) is a favorite pastime and way of

relaxing. It is often the central event of a social gathering. People invite their friends out for a sauna party, and the most enjoyable part is the "after-sauna". They relax either outdoors in front of the log cabin along the banks of a lake, or in an easy-chair in the living room before an open fire. After a sauna it is guaranteed that you will become very hungry and thirsty, and the Finns love to eat and drink together afterwards to replenish themselves.

Finnish food is food for people with simple taste and keen appetites. It is at

its best prepared in a straightforward and simple manner: splendid fresh trout and other fish from the lakes, slipped onto branches and roasted over an open fire; delicious Lapland salmon bound to planks and smoked before a fire; priceless fresh turbot caviar; the endless variety of mushrooms found in the woods that taste so delicious with sour cream; wild summer berries such as orange-red arctic brambleberries, and raspberries that have grown large and sweet and have soaked up the aroma of the bright Lapland summer nights.

From the countryside – Finland's well known Karelian pies, together with pickles, ham and the familiar home-made beer in a barrel.

The great party-time in Finland comes in August, at the opening of the crayfish season. Everywhere in Finland crayfish parties are organized, and heaps of these tiny, lobster-like creatures, boiled until fiery-red in richly spiced dill bouillon, are washed down with vodka.

Finns like their crayfish seasoned with dill.

Codfish lie on racks to dry in the long northern daylight and fresh salty sea breeze.

NORWAY

Nature blessed Norway with an overflowing abundance of mountains, rocky shores, fjords and virgin forests. It is the perfect place to enjoy fully the wonders of nature, but a hard place to live since only about 4% of the land can be cultivated. Norwegian cooking, therefore, is not very rich, but rather simple and hearty. Cooking depends heavily on two staples: fish and potatoes. In this land of endless coastlines fjords and mountain streams, the herring and cod, turbot and sole, salmon and trout are among the best to be found anywhere in the world. Because these fish can be bought while still alive, most Norwegians never consider fish eaten anywhere outside Norway fresh enough for their taste.

Norwegians have also discovered many ways to preserve their fish and their scarce supply of meat for long periods. Especially in the islands of the north and along the fjords, you can see long horizontal

14

Cool Scandinavian fjords provide fishermen with abundant catches.

bars hung with large pieces of cod to dry in the ice-cold, bone-dry, north wind. After two or three months, the cod is dry and as hard as a rock. It can be kept for years without going bad. Sometimes, cod is salted and then placed on rocks to dry. Norwegians call this "klippfisk".

Norwegian housewives make a special dish called "lutfisk" from the salted dry cod. This is done by soaking the cod for a few days in fresh water and then putting it in a mixture of water and birchwood ash so that it acquires a slightly rubbery consistency. Norwegians are very fond of this dish but to non-Scandinavians it seems on the bland side and must be garnished with healthy amounts of butter, cream and mustard to be enjoyed.

After the autumn slaughter, (there is not enough forage to keep animals through the winter) mutton is salted and smoked or hung out in the cold, freezing Norwegian wind for as

long as six months. After this curing process, it remains edible for years. (In the folklore museum at Oslo, there are legs of mutton preserved in this way that are said to be at least three hundred years old and still edible.)

To the list of delicious gastronomic specialties of Norway, knowledgeable gourmets add the royal salmon, the snow grouse and such game as elk, hare and above all, reindeer. A tender reindeer steak, fried in good country butter and accompanied by a compôte of woodland berries, is one of the most delectable dishes that can

be had anywhere in Scandinavia.

On many remote Norwegian farms, women still bake their own bread, and there is a vigorous spirit of competition between farmwives as to whose "flattbröd" is the thinnest and the crispiest. This dark crisp bread is the perfect companion not only for smoked reindeer but also for another Norwegian specialty: "Gjetost", a cheese made from goat's milk that has been simmered so long that it acquires a rust-brown, caramel color and a slightly sweet taste.

Breakfast in Norway is an extensive affair. The tourist staying in his first Norwegian hotel will be surprised to find such a fabulously laid-out table decked with numerous sorts of cold meat and fish, cheese, eggs, jam, compôtes and at least five different types of bread. Everyone can choose what he likes and as much as he likes. Hot coffee is served with milk. After such a breakfast Norwegians are understandably not very hungry at lunchtime, and they usually simply have a sandwich and a glass of milk. Early in the evening the members of the family gather around the large dinner table, on which, more often than not, fish is the special treat.

Summer in Scandinavia is brief but intense, with daylight hours that hardly seem to end and a sun that rises almost as soon as it has set. During this bright northern summer Scandinavians live out- *doors as much as they can, hardly seeming to take time even to sleep. They dance around the May Pole and Midsummer Night bonfires, picnic and walk and swim under the never darkening*

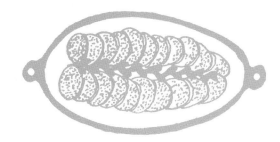

The Baltic Sea is renowned for a small but delectable herring found nowhere else. For centuries Swedish housewives have used this fish in preparing the most delicious dishes, soaking the herring in sweet and spicy sauces or in velvety smooth ones made from sweet and sour creams.

SWEDEN

"Rich Sweden" is a phrase often used enviously by the rest of Europe to describe this Scandinavian country. Its wealth and prosperity are displayed in the most enticing fashion in the Swedish "Smörgåsbord".

Smörgåsbord is also found in the other countries of Scandinavia, but it is never so abundant as in Sweden. It developed from a time when each guest at big country gatherings brought some food of his own. Today it is an immeasurably grander affair. With his plate in hand the guest serves himself from the richly laid out buffet, selecting just what he wants. This sort of meal reveals two very Swedish characteristics: first, their hearty appetites – each person can spoon out as much as he likes, as often as he pleases – and second, Swedish individualism – everyone chooses his own

place to enjoy the food, even alone in a corner if he feels like it.

The most elaborate smörgåsbord can be found in the luxury restaurants of Stockholm, Operakällaren and Stalmestergarden, where more than 60 different dishes are displayed on a beautifully decorated buffet table. But it would be wrong to think that you can just choose at random from the assortment. Quite the contrary! Everything is displayed together, but the guests follow certain unwritten rules.

Everyone invariably begins with herring. Delectable Baltic herring takes on a variety of shapes, forms and flavors: it can be marinated, smoked, sour, sweet-and-sour, in cream sauce, in piquant sauce, and on and on. After this, each person takes a clean plate and goes on to the second course which consists of cold fish: salmon or trout or some other fish prepared in aspic and ideally served with a cucumber salad. Then comes the cold-meat course: liver pâtés, roast beef, pork, and sometimes delicacies such as smoked

reindeer or other cold game. This is accompanie by a green salad with sou cream or a potato salad with a sweet-and-sour sauce of such woodland delights as bilberries, cloudberries or cranberries. Then it is tim to begin dishing out surprises from the containers kept warm ove a fondue burner. There are meatballs in gravy, spicy ragouts, sometimes even stewed bear or reindeer and often warm omelets or soufflés. Afterwards come cheeses and finally dessert or frui salad.

National beverages

*Beer, the national drink of
Denmark, is always good
accompanied by cheese and fruit.*

DENMARK

Beer is the national drink of Denmark, and there are so many different kinds you can choose a different beer for each hour of the day, for each mood and occasion. They range from strong "Easter" beers, which contain 8% alcohol, to very light, blond beers to quench a summer thirst.

The Danes also love Akvavit. It is usually drunk from small but elegant long-stemmed glasses, so cold that the glass itself becomes fogged. Akvavit must be downed in one large swallow. During the cold, damp Danish winter, people warm their bones with piping hot, strong coffee made even more potent with Akvavit. They drop a small shiny coin into the bottom of a coffee cup, pour in enough black coffee to make the coin disappear, and then pour in enough Akvavit to make the coin visible again, gleaming in the bottom of the cup.

FINLAND

In Finland, Akvavit is less popular than vodka. This is only one of the many signs of the century the country spent under Russian rule. (Some of the best features of Finnish cooking are the result of a unique blend of Russian and Scandinavian influences).

NORWAY

Norwegian Akvavit is truly the national beverage. In Norway, this potent liquor is made from unpeeled potatoes (hence the brown color) and flavored with caraway seeds. The finest brand is stored in huge sherry vats of oak, made of New Orleans oak or the American white oak, which are sent by cargo ship from Norway to Australia and back. It is said that the rolling of the ship combined with the change of climate when crossing the "Line" adds a striking flavor to the Akvavit.

Scotch is the most popular liquor in Norway although all are very expensive. Most liquor is imported, but the Wine Monopoly of Norway ("Vinmonopolet") concocts its own brands of Scotch and Gin which are sold at fairly reasonable prices and consequently bought in quantity by Norwegians. When ordering Scotch or Gin in Norway, remember to mention your favorite brand or else you may end up with something you don't like – which is the Norwegian witchcraft medicine.

Norwegians are great beer drinkers and the quality is good throughout the country. Norwegian beer is exported in great quantities to the United States and is one of the biggest sellers of foreign beer.

SWEDEN

Akvavit* (* or Aquavit from the latin aqua vitae) still bears the medieval name which has been traced back to the first distilled liquors produced from wine for medicinal purposes in France and Italy in the 13th century.

The first use of Akvavit was in connection with the manufacture of gunpowder. In 1498, the first licence to sell Akvavit in Stockholm was granted.

During the 16th century, Akvavit was produced merely by distilling wine, which had to be imported since wine grapes are not grown in Sweden. This turned out to be very expensive and Akvavit was therefore used mainly for medicinal purposes. During the dreaded plague at the end of the century, people began to use Akvavit, believing this new elixir had miraculous powers. Not until Swedish soldiers during the wars at the end of the 16th century had learned how to produce Akvavit from grain did it become a more common liquor.

In the 18th century it was discovered that potatoes were suitable for producing Akvavit, and from that time they have been the main source. Clean potatoes are boiled in steam under pressure. The resultant starch mass is mixed with crushed malt made from barley or mixed grains to convert the starch into sugar. Yeast cultures are then added to the mash, and in the ensuing fermentation the sugar is converted into alcohol. The mixture thus obtained has a very low percentage of alcohol, and contains other elements as well, removed by distillation.

In the modern distilling apparatus used in Sweden, the alcohol is separated from the fermented mash. The spirit from the potato distilleries is purified again in the distilleries before it is used to enter as an ingredient in the finished products such as Akvavit, punch or liqueur.

In Sweden, Akvavit (along with brandy or beer) is the natural drink with a Smörgåsbord. The guest pours his own drinks, sometimes from small decanters which stand on the buffet table; the Akvavit from bottles frozen into blocks of ice. Toasting with Akvavit is a ritual with fixed rules in Sweden. At very formal dinners you take the glass

in the right hand (men hold their glasses just above the top button of their jackets), look the person to whom the toast is directed in the eye and say "skål" bowing your head and emptying the glass in one swallow. Then you look each other in the eye again, in a little less solemn and more friendly way than before, nod and put the glass down.

Swedish punch has a high sugar content and a relatively low percentage of alcohol, in common with most liqueurs. In Sweden it is usually taken with coffee. Punch was first introduced in the 18th century when Swedish merchants began to trade with the East Indies. The liquor they brought home made from rice and sugar cane, is the basic ingredient in punch. Like other liquors, punch requires long ripening in oak vats to bring out its choicest qualities. As a curiosity, it may be mentioned that according to old Swedish usage, punch is sometimes taken warm with pea soup.

Danish open sandwiches

Open sandwiches are a Danish
national institution. The Danes
call these sandwiches simply
'smørrebrød', literally, bread and
butter, but anyone who has tried
any of these artfully arranged
sandwiches will know that three
or four pieces of smörrebröd are
more than enough to make an
elaborate and filling meal.
Danish restaurants have menus in
which the diner can choose from
literally hundreds of different

types of smørrebrød. The choice
is often baffling
Open sandwiches in a somewhat
simpler form (but no less
fancifully created) are taken to
work at the office for lunch and
children carry them to school in a
small tin lunch box, with 'eat
heartily' often inscribed on the
top. Smørrebrød are also perfect
for picnics.
Danish beer, exported to almost
every country in the world, goes

perfectly with smørrebrød. The
Danes often drink their beer
accompanied by a glass of
'akvavit', a clear, innocent
looking fluid, but a drink to be
treated with respect. Akvavit is
drunk from thimble-sized,
long-stemmed glasses filled to the
brim. First the sweet but strong
akvavit, and then a swallow of
beer – the perfect combination
with smørrebrød!

*A few of the many kinds of artis-
tically prepared open sandwiches.*

Danish Smørrebrød

Smorrebrod—breads

There is no more pleasant experience in eating than picking-and-choosing from the fantastic variety of small, beautiful and marvelously tasty sandwiches known as smorrebrod. They turn up as a first course, as a lunch, or, as the Danes like, in a full course meal—first fish, then meat and/or salad, then cheese. Both the art and the fun of making open sandwiches is variety—variety of color, flavor, texture. For you don't really make your sandwich—you compose it, as an artist plans a picture. First the base — and for that you need either dark rye or white bread, generously buttered, covered with a leaf of Boston lettuce.

Smorrebrod with fish

Start with dark rye bread and top with —

• Marinated herring with raw onion rings and a sprig of dill.
• Curried herring with chopped onions and capers.
• Smoked eel with scrambled eggs and a tomato wedge.
• Slices of hard boiled egg topped with a cone of smoked salmon filled with caviar and a sprig of dill.
• Slices of hard boiled egg covered with shrimps, mayonnaise and 2 lemon twists.

Start with white bread —

• Top with smoked salmon and dill or
• Tiny shrimps with mayonnaise, lemon and a sprig of dill.
• Serve Danish caviar on white toast. Make a ring of chopped onions on top, and place a raw egg yolk in the middle.
• Serve lobstertail salad in a small dish with mayonnaise, asparagus dipped in paprika and white toast on the side.

Smorrebrod with meat

Start with dark rye bread and top with —

• Sliced roast beef, slices of tomato and fried onions topped with a fried egg.
• Sliced roast beef topped with remoulade sauce, fried onions and cucumber salad with a wedge of tomato.
• Sliced roast beef, potato salad, finely chopped chives and 2 cucumber twists.
• A slice of ham topped with tomato slices and a fried egg.
• Pickled beef with meat aspic, onion rings, a wedge of tomato and parsley.
• Tartar with caviar topped with a raw egg yolk in an onion ring.
• Tartar with chopped pickle and onion, capers and freshly grated horseradish.
• Liverpaste (either sliced or spread) topped with fried mushrooms and 2 slices of bacon, served with tomato wedges and 2 cucumber twists.
• Overlapping slices of salami topped with a piece of aspic and onion rings with a tomato wedge and parsley.
• Chicken breast with mayonnaise, asparagus and a tomato wedge.

Warm open face sandwiches

In the case of warm open face sandwiches, the bread, usually dark rye, is served to the side and a leaf of Boston lettuce is underneath the topping —

• Warm fried fillet of plaice with remoulade sauce, lemon and tomato wedges, and a sprig of parsley.
• Warm fried codroe with remoulade sauce and lemon.
• Warm deep fried chicken breast with cucumber salad and a tomato wedge.
• Warm roast duckling with red cabbage, prunes and an orange twist.
• Warm farmer's sausage with red cabbage and cucumber salad.
• Warm pork tenderloin with onions and cucumber salad and tomato slices on the side.
• Warm Danish fried meatball with red cabbage and cucumber salad.
• Warm veal liver with bacon, fried onions and cucumber salad.

Smorrebrod with cheese

An assortment of Danish cheeses make delicious open face sandwiches to follow the meal. Danish brie and camembert, havarti, samsoe, maribo, elbo, esrom, mycella, bolina, Danish emmenthal and blue may all be served on a slice of generously buttered white bread. They should be arranged in slices, topped with either a twist of orange, red or green pepper slices, grapes or thin slices of radish.

Oliver Twist sandwich

Leverpostej

10 servings

- 4 *tablespoons margarine or*
  butter
- ½ *cup flour*
- 1 *cup milk*
- 1 *pound beef liver*
- ½ *pound salt pork*
- 1 *large onion*
- 1 *egg*
- 1 *teaspoon salt*
- ¼ *teaspoon black pepper*

Melt margarine in small
saucepan; blend in flour.
Gradually add milk, stirring
briskly until smooth. Cook over
medium heat stirring constantly
until thick and bubbly; cool.
Cut liver, pork and onion into
small pieces. Puree in small
amounts in blender at high
speed or put through food
grinder. Stir pureed mixture into
white sauce; blend well. Add
egg, salt and pepper; mix well.
Pour into a well buttered
9″ × 5″ × 3″ baking dish.
Cover top with foil, sealing
edges tightly. Place in large
baking pan. Pour boiling water
into baking pan to a depth of
2″. Bake in a 350° oven 1 hour.
Remove from oven and lift
off cover. Cool. Store covered
in refrigerator. Serve in ½″ slices.

Hans Christian Andersen sandwich

Smørrebrød H. C. Andersen

4 servings

- 4 *slices rye or pumpernickel*
  bread
  Margarine or butter
- 4 *slices liver paté*
- 8 *slices liverwurst*
- 1 *tomato, sliced*
- 8 *cooked bacon curls*
- 4 *pickles, cut into fans*
  Lettuce leaves

Spread bread generously with
margarine; top with liver paté.
Garnish with tomato, bacon
curls and pickles. Serve on
lettuce leaves.

Danish liver paté

Smørrebrød Oliver Twist

6 servings

- 6 *slices pumpernickel bread*
  Margarine or butter
- 6 *slices cooked ham*
- 1 *tablespoon horseradish*
- ½ *cup whipped cream or*
- ½ *cup sour cream*
- 12 *cooked pitted prunes*
- 6 *orange slices*

Spread bread with margarine.
Place folded slice of ham on
bread. Stir horseradish into
whipped cream. Heap spoonful
of cream in center of ham.
Place a prune on either side of
cream. Cut orange slices halfway
and twist; place in center of
cream. Serve immediately.

Danish fondue

Fondue Dansk

4 servings

  1 clove garlic, cut in half
1½ cups Danish beer
  1 pound Creamy Havarti
      cheese, shredded
  2 tablespoons dry mustard
      Salt and pepper
  1 loaf firm-crusted bread, cut
      into cubes

Rub garlic all over the inside of an earthenware fondue pot. Place over low heat and pour in the beer. Heat to bubbling. Toss the cheese with combined flour and mustard. Add cheese mixture to beer, a handful at a time, stirring constantly over low heat as if making a figure 8. When mixture is creamy and smooth add salt and pepper. Place fondue pot over a portable burner at the table. Using a long-handled fork, dip bread cubes into fondue.

Danish beer and Creamy Havarti cheese are combined to make this delicious variation on an old Swiss favorite.

Swedish Smörgåsbord

Looking like a brilliant abstract painting, this collection of containers and jars holds an almost limitless variety of appetizing Scandinavian seafood delicacies.

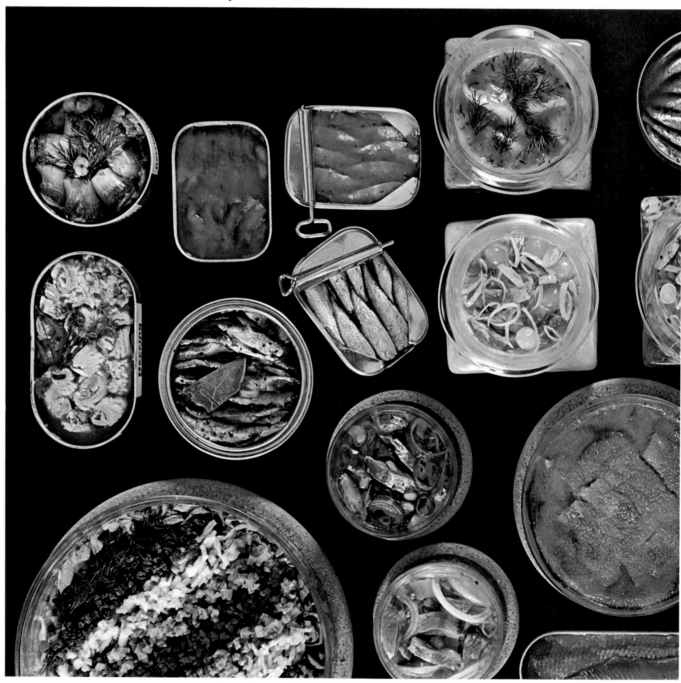

People the world over have heard of the Swedish smörgåsbord. In fact, the other countries of Scandinavia also enjoy this buffet table on which a choice of delicious dishes are displayed. But in Sweden, the smörgåsbord appears in its richest and most elaborate form. From a festively laid table, each person can choose from the best the land and sea have to offer. First fish dishes, then salads, then both cold and hot meat and pâtés, and finally cheese or a fruit compote. Of all the endless variations brought to the table, the most elaborate come with the fish dishes. The 'sillbord', an enormous choice of seafood delicacies with herring as their basis, is a Swedish discovery (or at least so declare the Swedes with pride). The fish is marinated, salted, fried, smoked and often find a place in salads. The hospitable Swedes want everyone to enjoy something from the inexhaustible riches of the sea. And nothing tastes better with this sillbord than a good glass of Swedish akvavit.

Herring pudding

Sillpudding

4 to 6 servings

  1 *salted regular or schmalz herring (about ¾ to 1 pound)*
  2 *tablespoons margarine or butter*
1½ *cups thinly sliced onion*
  3 *cups cooked potatoes, peeled and sliced*
  ¼ *teaspoon ground white pepper*
  2 *eggs*
  2 *tablespoons flour*
1¾ *cups milk*

Soak herring in cold water 24 hours; skin and fillet; cut into ½″ strips. Melt margarine in large skillet, add onions and cook until transparent, stirring occasionally. Add potatoes; cook, stirring occasionally, until heated through, about 10 minutes. Place half the potatoes and onion mixture in bottom of greased 9 inch round (2 inches high) baking pan. Arrange herring pieces over potatoes, sprinkle with pepper; cover with remaining potato mixture. Combine eggs, flour and milk; beat until just blended, not foamy; pour over potatoes. Place pan in larger baking pan. Pour boiling water in outside pan to a depth of 1″ on smaller pan. Bake in a hot oven (425°) until top is browned and custard is set, about 30 to 40 minutes. Serve hot.

Herring in sherry pickle

Sherrysill

4 servings

  2 *salted schmalz herring filleted and skinned*
  ⅓ *cup sherry wine*
  ¼ *cup water*
  3 *tablespoons vinegar*
  ½ *cup sugar*
  ¼ *teaspoon ground allspice or*
  3 *allspice berries, crushed*
  2 *onions, thinly sliced*
     Chopped fresh dill

Cover herring with cold water; soak 24 hours. Drain and rinse. Place in a non-metallic bowl. Combine sherry, water, vinegar, sugar and allspice; pour over herring. Refrigerate about 24 hours. Serve garnished with sliced onions and dill.

Danish pickled salted herring

Inlagd sild

4 servings

  2 *salted schmalz herring, filleted and skinned*
  2 *medium onions, sliced*
  ½ *cup vinegar*
  ⅔ *cup water*
  1 *cup sugar*
 10 *allspice berries, crushed*

Cover fillets with cold water; soak 24 hours. Drain and rinse; cut into ½″ pieces. Place in non-metallic bowl or glass jar. Combine remaining ingredients and bring to a boil; cool; pour over herring. Refrigerate several hours or overnight before serving.

Danish herring au gratin

Sildgratin

6 servings

  2 *schmalz or matjes herring fillets*
  4 *tablespoons margarine or butter*
  1 *tablespoon chopped onion*
  3 *tablespoons flour*
  2 *cups half-and-half*
  ½ *teaspoon salt*
  ¼ *teaspoon ground white pepper*
  2 *tablespoons chopped parsley*
  6 *small cooked potatoes, peeled and sliced*
  2 *hard cooked eggs, chopped*
  2 *tablespoons grated Parmesan cheese*
  1 *tablespoon margarine or butter*

Soak fillets in cold water for 24 hours; drain. Cut fillets into ½″strips. Melt margarine in saucepan, add onion and cook until transparent. Stir in flour; remove from heat; gradually add half-and-half. Cook over medium heat, stirring constantly, until mixture comes to a boil and is thickened. Stir in salt, pepper and parsley. Butter 6 individual casserole dishes; arrange 1 sliced potato in bottom of each, cover with half the sauce. Divide chopped egg and herring evenly among the casseroles, top with remaining sauce. Sprinkle with Parmesan cheese; dot with margarine. Bake in very hot oven (450°) about 15 minutes, or until bubbly and top is lightly browned.

Danish marinated salmon

Gravad laks

6 servings

- *2 tablespoons salt*
- *2 tablespoons sugar*
- *1 tablespoon peppercorns, crushed*
- *2 teaspoons fennel seed*
- *1 pound salmon, cut into 2 fillets*
- *1 large bunch fresh dill, chopped coarsely*

Combine salt, sugar, fennel and pepper. Place fish on large piece heavy duty foil. Cover fish with dill; sprinkle with salt mixture. Top with second fish fillet. Close foil securely using a drug store wrap; place on dish or tray. Pile several weights or 3 or 4 cans of food on foil packet. Refrigerate at least 48 hours turning packet several times. Be sure to keep weights on packet. Remove fish; scrape off seasonings. Slice thinly and serve with salmon sauce or **Danish mustard sauce** (recipes page 41).

Danish marinated herring

Gravad sild

4 servings

- *4 herring or trout, about 6-ounces each*
- *4 tablespoons dill weed*
- *6 tablespoons vegetable oil*
- *⅔ cup vinegar*
- *2 teaspoons salt*
- *1 tablespoon sugar*
- *½ teaspoon ground white pepper*
- *1 teaspoon dry mustard*

Fillet fish and remove skin. Place alternate layers of fish and dill in a non-metallic bowl. Combine and beat with a fork oil, vinegar, salt, sugar, pepper and mustard; pour over fish. Cover bowl; refrigerate for several hours or overnight.

Danish caviar

Hjemmelavet kaviar

- *Danish caviar*
- *Lemon wedges*
- *Chopped onion*
- *Chopped egg*
- *Sour cream*
- *Butter*
- *Pumpernickel bread*
- *Hot toast*

Serve caviar in a bowl of ice. Surround caviar with lemon wedges, chopped onion, chopped egg, sour cream and butter all in separate bowls or serving dishes. Place bread and toast in serving dishes or baskets. Serve chilled aquavit, vodka or champagne, if desired.

Finnish pickled herring

Etikkasilliä

4 servings

- *4 salted herring, filleted and skinned*
- *2 cups vinegar*
- *1 cup water*
- *½ cup sugar*
- *3 bay leaves*
- *1 2" piece ginger root, sliced thinly*
- *2 teaspoons mustard seed*
- *1 tablespoon prepared horseradish*
- *4 small red onions, thinly sliced*
- *1 carrot, thinly sliced*

Soak herring in cold water at least 24 hours in a cool place. Drain; cut into ½" strips. Combine vinegar, water and sugar; bring to a boil over moderate heat. Simmer about 5 minutes until syrupy. In a non-metallic bowl, make alternate layers of herring, bay leaves, ginger root, mustard seed, horseradish, sliced onions and carrots. Pour vinegar syrup over fish; cover; refrigerate for 3 days.

Danish marinated salmon

Salads

Finnish herring salad

Rosolli

4 to 6 servings

  1 *salted regular or schmalz*
     herring (about 1 pound)
½ *cup whipped cream*
  1 *tablespoon pickled beet juice*
½ *teaspoon sugar*
  1 *teaspoon vinegar*
  2 *cups cold, cooked potatoes,*
     coarsely diced
  2 *cups cold, cooked carrots,*
     coarsely diced
  1 *(1 pound) can beets, drained*
     and coarsely diced
  2 *medium, tart apples, peeled,*
     cored and diced
  1 *large pickle, coarsely diced*
  2 *hard cooked eggs, coarsely*
     chopped
½ *tablespoon finely chopped*
     onion
     Parsley or watercress sprigs

Soak herring in cold water for
24 hours; skin and fillet.
Combine whipped cream, beet
juice, sugar and vinegar; chill.
Cut herring into cubes; combine
with remaining ingredients,
except parsley; mix well. Fold in
whipped cream dressing. Chill.
Serve garnished with parsley or
watercress.

Swedish pickled beets

Inkokta rödbetor

4 servings

  4 *pounds small beets (about*
     4 bunches)
2½ *cups boiling water*
  1 *cup vinegar*
1½ *teaspoons salt*
  1 *cup sugar*
10 *cloves*
10 *peppercorns*
  2 *teaspoons horseradish*

Cook beets until tender; peel
under running cold water. In a
saucepan, mix hot water,
vinegar, sugar, cloves,
peppercorns, and horseradish.
Place cooked beets in a 3 quart
casserole. Pour in hot pickling
mixture. Cover with plastic wrap
and cool. Refrigerate overnight.

Danish pickled cucumbers

Syltede agurker

6 to 8 servings

  3 *medium cucumbers*
½ *cup vinegar*
½ *cup water*
  2 *tablespoons sugar*
  1 *teaspoon salt*
¼ *teaspoon ground white*
     pepper

Peel cucumbers, if desired;
slice very thinly into serving
bowl. Combine remaining
ingredients; beat with fork.
Pour over cucumbers. Cover;
chill at least one hour before
serving.

Danish herring salad

Sildsalat

6 servings

  2 *salted regular or schmalz*
     herring
  3 *medium cooked potatoes,*
     peeled and diced
  2 *small cooked or canned*
     beets, diced
  1 *large pickle, diced*
  2 *medium tart apples, peeled,*
     cored and diced
½ *cup cooked ham, tongue or*
     corned beef, diced
  2 *tablespoons finely chopped*
     onion
  2 *tablespoons margarine or*
     butter
  2 *tablespoons flour*
1¼ *cups half-and-half*
  1 *tablespoon vinegar*
  1 *teaspoon prepared mustard*
½ *teaspoon salt*
     Pinch of sugar

Soak herring overnight in cold
water; skin and fillet. Cut herring
into ½″ pieces. Combine
with potatoes, beets, pickle,
apple, meat and onion. Chill.
Melt margarine in saucepan;
stir in flour. Remove from heat;
stir in half-and-half, vinegar,
mustard, salt and sugar. Cook
over medium heat, stirring
constantly, until mixture comes
to a boil and is thickened.
Carefully stir into salad mixture;
chill. Serve on lettuce, garnished
with additional hard-cooked
egg slices, if desired.

*Salted herring and sweet beets
produce the unique Scandinavian
flavor of Danish herring salad.*

Swedish Westcoast salad

Västkustsallad

4 servings

> 1 (6½ ounce) can lobster
> 1 (10 ounce) can whole
>   clams, drained
> 1 cup cooked shrimp, peeled
> 1 (3 ounce) can sliced
>   mushrooms
> ¼ cup mayonnaise
> ¼ cup sour cream
> 1 tablespoon lemon juice
> ½–1 teaspoon salt
>   Lettuce leaves
> 2 tomatoes, quartered

Drain lobster and remove membranes. Combine lobster, clams, shrimp, mushrooms, mayonnaise, sour cream, lemon juice and salt; toss lightly until mixed. Arrange salad on lettuce leaves. Garnish with tomato wedges.

Danish curried lobster salad

Hummersalat

4 servings

> 1 (6½ ounce) can lobster
> ¼ cup mayonnaise
> ¼ cup sour cream
> 1 teaspoon lemon juice
> ½ teaspoon curry powder
> 2 stalks celery, chopped
> 1 apple, cored and diced
>   Lettuce leaves
> 2 hard cooked eggs, quartered

Drain lobster and remove membranes. Combine mayonnaise, sour cream, lemon juice and curry; blend until smooth. Add celery, apple and mayonnaise mixture to lobster; toss lightly. Pile salad lightly in lettuce leaves; garnish with egg wedges.

Danish fish salad

Fisksalat

4 servings

> ½ cup mayonnaise
> 2 teaspoons prepared mustard
> 2 tablespoons lemon juice
> ¾ pound cooked, flaked cod or
>   other white fish
>   Lettuce leaves
> 1 hard cooked egg, sliced
>   Watercress or dill

Combine mayonnaise, mustard and lemon juice. Carefully stir in flaked fish; chill. Serve on lettuce leaves; garnish with hard-cooked egg slices and watercress or dill.

Swedish crab salad

Krabbsallad

4 servings

> 1 (6½ ounce) can crabmeat
> 2 stalks celery, chopped
> 1 teaspoon grated onion
> 1–2 tablespoons lemon juice
> ¼ teaspoon dill weed
> ½ cup sour cream
>   Freshly ground black peppe
>   Lettuce leaves

Drain crabmeat and remove membranes. Combine crabmeat celery, onion, lemon juice, dill, sour cream, and pepper. Toss lightly; arrange salad on lettuce

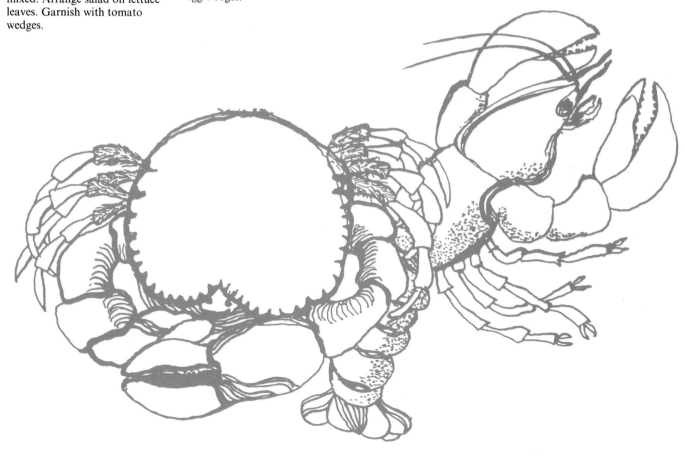

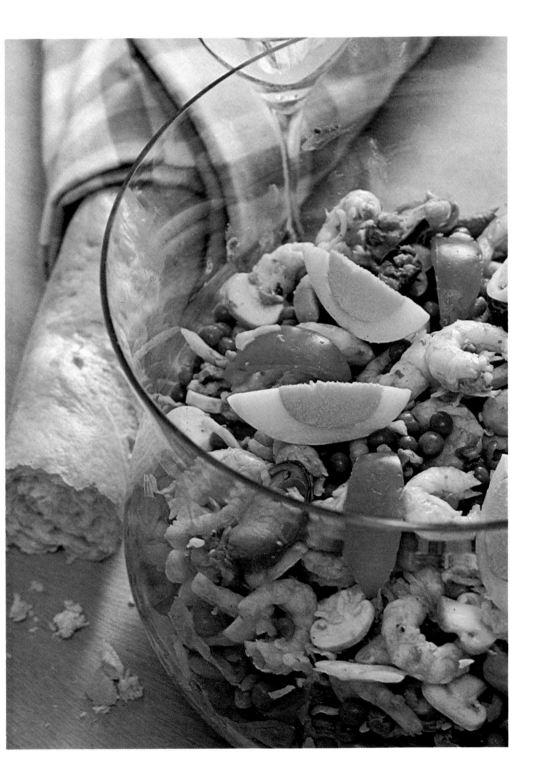

Joppes räksallad

4 servings

> 1   pound shrimp, cooked and peeled
> 2½ cups sliced fresh mushrooms
> 2   medium tomatoes, quartered
> 1   cup peas, cooked and drained
> 2   tablespoons oil
> 2   teaspoons vinegar
> ½ teaspoon salt
> ¼ teaspoon dill weed
> 2   hard cooked eggs, cut in wedges

Arrange shrimp, mushrooms, **tomatoes and cold peas** in salad bowl. Combine oil, vinegar, salt and dill; pour over salad mixture. Garnish with egg wedges.

Joppe's shrimp salad. Denmark's small delicate shrimp have a sweet and salty taste. They are so delicious that no gourmet would ever think of covering them with mayonnaise.

Danish beet salad

Rödbedesalat

4 to 6 servings

   1 *(16 ounce) jar pickled beets,*
    drained
   2 *medium apples, thinly sliced*
   ½ *cup mayonnaise*

Combine sliced beets and apples;
stir in mayonnaise. Chill well.
Serve with cold meat or smoked
fish.

Swedish cabbage and cranberry salad

Vitkåls- och lingonsallad

4 servings

   1 *cup finely shredded cabbage*
   ¾ *cup whole cranberry sauce*
   1 *tablespoon lemon juice*
   ¼ *teaspoon salt.*

Combine cabbage, cranberry
sauce, lemon juice, and salt;
toss lightly. Chill thoroughly.

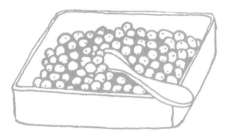

Swedish carrot and apple salad

Morots- och äppelsallad

4 servings

   2 *large carrots, grated*
   2 *medium apples, grated*
   1 *tablespoon lemon juice*

Combine carrots, apples, and
lemon juice; toss lightly. Chill
thoroughly. Serve with fish
dishes.

Danish red cabbage salad

Rödkaalssalat

4 servings

   1 *cup finely shredded red*
    cabbage
   2 *medium apples, coarsely*
    grated
   1 *medium onion, chopped*
   1 *teaspoon caraway seed,*
    crushed
   2 *tablespoons French dressing*

Combine all ingredients; toss
lightly.

Norwegian raw vegetable medley

Råkostkabarét

4 to 6 servings

   1 *cup finely shredded cabbage*
   2 *cooked beets, coarsely grated*
   2 *carrots, coarsely grated*
   1 *apple, peeled and grated*
   1 *tablespoon lemon juice*
   ½ *cup mayonnaise*
   2 *tablespoons milk*

Combine cabbage, beets, carrots,
and grated apple; mix in lemon
juice. Blend mayonnaise with
milk; add to vegetables and toss
to mix well. (If preferred, group
vegetables separately and serve
mayonnaise dressing in separate
dish.)

Swedish cabbage and apple salad

Vitkåls- och äppelsallad

4 servings

   2 *cups shredded Savoy cabbage*
   2 *medium apples, sliced*
   ¼ *cup orange juice*
   ¼ *teaspoon salt*
   1 *tablespoon lemon juice*
   ½ *cup cream, whipped*

Combine shredded cabbage,
apple slices, orange juice, lemon
juice, and salt; mix well.
Carefully stir in whipped
cream. Chill.

Swedish cabbage and orange salad

Vitkåls- och apelsinsallad

4 servings

   1 *cup finely shredded white*
    cabbage
   2 *naval oranges, sectioned*
   ¼ *cup raisins*
   1 *tablespoon salad oil*
   1 *tablespoon lemon juice*

Combine cabbage, oranges, and
raisins. Add oil and lemon juice;
toss well. Chill thoroughly.
Serve with meat and fish dishes.

Danish stuffed tomatoes

Tomater med fyld

6 servings

   1 *(1 pound) jar pickled*
    schmalz herring
   2 *tart apples, peeled, cored*
    and diced
   ½ *cup mayonnaise*
  1½ *teaspoons dried dill weed*
   ¼ *teaspoon salt*
   ⅛ *teaspoon ground white pepper*
   2 *tablespoons cream or*
    half-and-half
   6 *medium tomatoes*
    Parsley or dill sprigs

Drain herring; chop. Combine
herring, apple, mayonnaise, dill
weed, salt, pepper and cream.
Remove stem end from
tomatoes; carefully remove
seeds and juice. Fill tomatoes
with herring salad mixture.
Serve cold, garnished with
sprig of parsley or dill.

Soups

Swedish meat soup

Köttsoppa

6 servings

 2 pounds soup meat
 3 quarts water
 2 medium carrots, coarsely
 diced
 1 turnip, cut into ½″ cubes
 1 stalk celery, diced
 1 medium onion, spiked with
 2 cloves
 2 scallions or leeks, sliced
 2 teaspoons salt
 1 teaspoon white pepper

Place meat in large saucepan; add water. Bring to a boil; skim. Add salt; reduce heat and simmer about 2 hours. Add carrot, turnip, celery, onion and scallions; sprinkle with salt and pepper. Bring to a boil again; reduce heat and simmer 1 hour. Remove meat, cut into pieces, return to soup and heat thoroughly.

Danish brown cabbage soup

Brunkaalsuppe

4 servings

 ½ cup margarine or butter
 1 small head cabbage,
 shredded
 1 tablespoon sugar
 2 (10½ ounce) cans beef
 consomme
 2 cans water
 1 teaspoon salt
 ½ teaspoon pepper
 1 tablespoon chopped parsley

In a large saucepan, melt margarine. Add cabbage; stir frequently, until cabbage is coated with margarine. Sprinkle with sugar; saute over low heat 3 minutes, stirring occasionally. Add consomme, water, salt and pepper. Cover; simmer over low heat about 20 minutes or until cabbage is tender. Sprinkle with parsley before serving.

Danish chervil soup

Körvelsuppe

4 servings

 ½ pound young carrots,
 scraped
 4 cups chicken bouillon
 3 tablespoons margarine or
 butter
 3 tablespoons flour
 4 tablespoons chopped chervil
 ½ teaspoon salt
 ¼ teaspoon pepper
 Croutons

Cook whole carrots in bouillon for 10 to 15 minutes or until tender. Strain; reserve bouillon; puree carrots. In a heavy saucepan, melt margarine, stir in flour; gradually add bouillon, stirring constantly. Cook 5 minutes; add pureed carrots and chervil; stir well. Add salt and pepper. Sprinkle with croutons just before serving.

Finnish pea soup

Hernekeitto

6 servings

 ¾ pound green split peas
 8 cups water
 1 ham hock or ham bone
 1 carrot, chopped
 1 medium onion, chopped
 2 teaspoons salt
 ½–1 teaspoon pepper

Soak peas in water about 12 hours. In a large pan, bring peas to boil in same water; skim. Add meat, carrot, and onion; simmer about 2 hours, or until peas are tender. Remove ham bone; return any pieces of ham to soup. Add salt and pepper.

Swedish meat soup

Norwegian cauliflower puree

Blomkålspuré

4 servings

 1 *large cauliflower*
 2 *cups water*
 1 *tablespoon margarine or*
   butter
1½ *tablespoons flour*
 4 *chicken bouillon cubes*
 4 *cups boiling water*
 ½ *teaspoon salt*
 ¼ *teaspoon white pepper*
 1 *egg yolk, beaten*
 ¼ *cup heavy cream*

Trim and wash cauliflower;
separate into flowerets. In a
large saucepan, cover cauliflower
with salted water, bring to a
boil and cook 10 minutes. Drain
and puree cauliflower in blender.
Melt margarine in small
saucepan; stir in flour until well
blended. Dissolve bouillon cubes
in boiling water; gradually stir
into margarine mixture. Cook,
stirring constantly, until slightly
thickened. Stir in pureed
cauliflower, salt and pepper.
In a small bowl, mix egg yolk
with heavy cream and 2 or 3
tablespoons of the hot soup.
Blend well, and stir into soup.
Serve hot.

Norrlandsk salmon soup

Norrländsk laxsoppa

4 servings

 5 *cups liquid (drain liquid*
   from can of salmon; add
   water to make 5 cups)
 3 *tablespoons barley*
 2 *medium carrots, diced*
 1 *medium turnip, diced*
 1 *medium onion, chopped*
 1 *(16-ounce) can pink salmon*
 1 *teaspoon salt*
   Dash black pepper
 2 *tablespoons chopped parsley*

Bring salmon liquid and water
to a boil. Add barley, boil 30
minutes. Add vegetables and
cook for 10–15 minutes, or until
tender. Add salmon pieces and
salt and pepper. Heat
thoroughly. Top with chopped
parsley. Serve hot.

Swedish bread soup

Ölsupa

4 servings

 3 *tablespoons margarine or*
   butter
 1 *tablespoon flour*
 4 *cups beef bouillon*
1½ *cups dry pumpernickel*
   bread crumbs
 1 *tablespoon sugar*
 4 *small cooked sausages,*
   chopped
 ¼ *cup heavy cream*

In a heavy saucepan melt
margarine; stir in flour.
Gradually add hot bouillon,
stirring constantly. Add
pumpernickel bread crumbs and
sugar. Cook over low heat about
30 minutes. Warm sausages in
the soup during last 5 minutes
of cooking. Stir in the cream;
serve immediately.

Danish pea soup

Gule aerter

8 servings

 1 *pound yellow split peas*
 3 *pints water*
 3 *pounds lightly salted pork*
 4 *pints water*
 3 *carrots*
 1 *piece celeriac*
 3 *leeks*
 3 *onions*
 8 *potatoes*
   Fresh or dried thyme to
   taste

Rinse the peas and soak
overnight in cold water. Boil
until tender in a
thick-bottomed saucepan
about 1¼ hours. Meanwhile,
boil the meat with the
vegetables and thyme until
tender. Puree peas through a
strainer. Strain the meat and
vegetables, and pour the
liquid into the puree. Bring to
a boil. Put all the vegetables
back into the soup, and serve
the meat either cold or warm
with the soup, accompanied
by farmer's sausage and
bread.

Danish pea soup

Norwegian fish soup

Fiskesuppe

4 servings

- 2 tablespoons margarine or butter
- 2 leeks or scallions, sliced
- 4 medium potatoes, diced
- 1 stalk celery, diced
- 2 teaspoons salt
- 1 teaspoon black pepper
- 5 cups water
- 1 pound fresh or frozen fish fillets
- 1 tablespoon chopped fresh dill or
- 1 teaspoon dried dill

In a large, heavy skillet melt margarine; saute leeks, potatoes and celery about 5 minutes over low heat. Add salt, pepper, and water; bring to a boil and cook about 10 to 15 minutes or until vegetables are tender. Cut fish fillets into 1-inch pieces; add to soup about 10 minutes before vegetables are tender. Correct seasoning and sprinkle with dill. Serve immediately.

Finnish fish soup

Kalakeitto

4 servings

- 2 medium potatoes, peeled and cubed
- 2 cups water
- 1 teaspoon salt
- 1 pound frozen haddock fillets, cut into bite size pieces
- 3 tablespoons margarine or butter
- 2 tablespoons flour
- 2 cups milk
  Dash white pepper
- 2 tablespoons chopped fresh dill

Cook potatoes in salted water about 10 minutes; add fish; simmer 15 minutes. In the meantime, melt margarine in saucepan. Stir in flour; add milk gradually, stirring constantly. Add to soup and cook, stirring constantly, for another 3 minutes. Top with chopped dill.

Swedish vegetable soup

Grönsakssoppa

4 to 6 servings

- 1 onion, chopped
- 3 carrots, sliced
- 3 tablespoons margarine or butter
- 5 cups hot water
- 1 beef bouillon cube
- 3 potatoes, peeled and diced
- 2 leeks or scallions, sliced
- ½ head cauliflower, divided into flowerets
- 4 stalks celery, chopped
- 2 teaspoons salt
- ½ teaspoon white pepper

In a heavy saucepan, saute onion and carrots in margarine until onion is transparent. Add water, bouillon cube, potatoes, leeks, cauliflower, celery, salt, and pepper. Cover; cook over low heat 15 to 20 minutes or until vegetables are tender.

Swedish spinach soup

Spenatsoppa

4 servings

- 1 (10½ ounce) can cream of chicken soup
- 1 cup milk
- 2 cups boiling water
- 2 chicken bouillon cubes
- 1 (10 ounce) package frozen chopped spinach, thawed
- 1 teaspoon salt
- ¼ teaspoon pepper
- 2 tablespoons chopped parsley
- 2 hard-cooked eggs

In a large saucepan, combine soup, milk, and boiling water in which bouillon cubes have been dissolved. Add spinach. Place mixture in blender for a few seconds on medium speed just until spinach is very finely chopped; do not puree. Return to saucepan; simmer 10 minutes. Add salt and pepper. Garnish with chopped parsley and quarters of hard-cooked eggs.

Swedish spinach soup

Finntastic soup

"Finntastinen"

4 servings

- 2 tablespoons butter
  or margarine
- ¼ cup chopped onion
- ¼ cup minced ham
- 1 can (10½ ounces)
  condensed cream of potato
  soup
- 1 soup can milk
- ⅛ teaspoon dill weed
- 1 cup shredded Swiss cheese

In saucepan, melt butter. Add onion and ham and cook until onion is tender. Gradually blend in soup and milk. Heat, stirring occasionally, until soup is hot. Do not boil. Add dill. Garnish each serving with cheese.

Danish apple soup

Aeblesuppe

4 servings

- 5 medium apples, unpeeled
- 4 cups water
- ½ teaspoon grated lemon rind
- 2 tablespoons cornstarch
- ¼ cup cold water
- ½ cup white wine
- ½ cup sugar
- 1 teaspoon cinnamon

Quarter apples, simmer in water with grated lemon rind for 5 minutes; strain. Add cornstarch which has been dissolved in cold water, stirring constantly. Add wine, sugar, and cinnamon; simmer 5 minutes. Serve hot or cold.

Skansk cabbage soup

Skånsk kålsoppa

4 servings

- 1 small (about 1 pound)
  smoked pork shoulder
- 6 cups water
- 1 bay leaf
- 5 peppercorns
- 5 allspice berries
- 1 small head cabbage (about
  1 pound), shredded
- 2 medium carrots, sliced
- 4 medium potatoes, cut into
  ½" cubes
- 2 scallions, sliced
- 1 teaspoon salt
  Dash pepper
  Chopped parsley

In a saucepan, bring the water to a boil, add the pork and reduce heat. Skim off fat. Add bay leaf, peppercorns and allspice; simmer about 30 minutes. Add vegetables; cook until tender. Remove pork and cut into pieces. Return to soup. Add pepper and salt. Sprinkle with parsley before serving.

Finnish summer soup

Kesäkeitto

6 to 8 servings

- 2½ cups water
- 1 tablespoon sugar
- 2½ cups milk
- 1 (10 ounce) package frozen
  peas
- ½ head cauliflower, cut into
  flowerets
- 1 medium carrot, diced
- 5 small potatoes, peeled and
  quartered
- 1 egg yolk
- 2 tablespoons margine or
  butter
- 1 tablespoon chopped chervil or
  parsley
  Salt to taste

In a large saucepan, bring water and sugar to a boil. Add the milk, peas, cauliflower, carrot and potatoes; simmer 10–15 minutes, or until vegetables are tender. Stir 2–3 tablespoons of hot soup into beaten egg yolk, then return to soup. Stir in margarine and chervil or parsley. Add salt last or soup will become lumpy. Serve immediately.

Finntastic soup

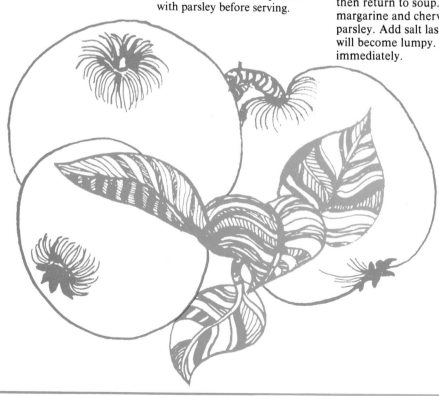

Vegetable dishes

Finnish creamed carrots

Kermaanmuhennetut porkkanat

4 servings

- 2 tablespoons margarine or butter
- 3 tablespoons flour
- 1 tablespoon sugar
  Dash of ground white pepper
- 1 cup milk
- ½ cup half-and-half
- 1 (1 pound) can sliced carrots, drained
  Chopped parsley

Melt margarine; add flour, sugar and pepper. Stir until well-blended. Remove from heat, slowly add milk and half-and-half; return to heat. Simmer, stirring constantly, until thickened. Add drained carrots; heat. Garnish with chopped parsley.

Creamed cauliflower

Stuved blomkål

4 servings

- 1 head cauliflower, parboiled
- 4 tablespoons butter
- 5 tablespoons flour
- 1 pint milk
  Salt and white pepper
  Dash nutmeg
  Finely chopped parsley

Melt the butter. Stir in flour till smooth. Remove from heat and add milk. Return to heat and stir constantly until smooth and thickened. Season. Break cauliflower into large flowerets and arrange in an ovenproof dish. Pour the sauce over and heat through in a hot oven for 5 minutes. Sprinkle with chopped parsley before serving.

Finnish turnip

Lanttu

4 to 6 servings

- 2 tablespoons margarine or butter
- 2 pounds yellow turnip, peeled and cut into ½" cubes
- 2 teaspoons salt
- 2 beef bouillon cubes
- 2 cups boiling water
  Parsley

Melt margarine in 2-quart saucepan. Sauté turnip cubes over medium heat, turning occasionally to brown lightly on all sides. Sprinkle with salt; add bouillon cubes and water. Bring to a boil; cover, reduce heat and simmer until tender about 25 minutes. Garnish with parsley.

Norwegian fried onions

Stekt lök

4 servings

- 2 tablespoons margarine or butter
- 4 medium onions, peeled and thinly sliced
- 1 teaspoon salt
- 1 teaspoon Worcestershire sauce
- 1 tablespoon chopped parsley

In large frying pan, melt margarine, add onions and salt; saute over medium heat, stirring occasionally, until transparent and golden brown Stir in Worcestershire sauce. Sprinkle with parsley before serving.

Finnish turnip

The turnip is a substantial and wholesome vegetable that goes well with a choice cut of pork.

38

Mashed Swedes

Rotmos

4 to 6 servings

1 pound yellow turnips, peeled
  and cut into ½" cubes
2 beef bouillon cubes
2 cups boiling water
½ teaspoon salt
⅛ teaspoon ground white pepper
⅛ teaspoon ground allspice
1½ pounds potatoes, peeled and
  cut into ½" cubes

Place turnip cubes into 2-quart
saucepan. Add bouillon cubes,
water, salt, pepper and allspice.
Boil about 15 minutes or until
half-cooked; add potatoe cubes;
cook 15 minutes more or until
tender. Drain and mash
vegetables; if needed, add a
little of the drained liquid.

Finnish beet steaks

Punajuuripihvit

4 servings

1 (1 pound) can sliced beets,
  drained
1 egg, lightly beaten
½ cup fine dry bread crumbs
2 tablespoons margarine or
  butter
1 tablespoon lemon juice
1 tablespoon chopped parsley

Dip beets in beaten egg. Sprinkle
half of bread crumbs on paper
towels; place beet slices on
crumbs and sprinkle with
remaining crumbs. Melt
margarine in skillet. Sauté beet
slices, turning to brown each
side. Place on platter, sprinkle
with lemon juice and parsley.

Danish braised cabbage

Rödkål

6 servings

4 tablespoons margarine or
  butter
2 pounds white cabbage,
  shredded
1 beef bouillon cube
1 cup boiling water
2 tablespoons maple or dark
  corn syrup
⅓ cup vinegar
½ teaspoon salt

In a large heavy saucepan, melt
margarine. Lightly brown
cabbage over moderately high
heat, turning frequently, about
5 minutes. Dissolve bouillon
cube in water. Add to cabbage
with syrup, vinegar, and salt;
toss with fork to blend. Cover;
cook over medium heat about
45 minutes or until cabbage is
tender. Remove cover during
last 10 minutes to allow any
excess liquid to evaporate. Serve
with Christmas ham or cooked
pork sausages.

Dilled peas Helsinki

Tilliherneet

4 servings

2 (10 ounce) packages green
  peas, cooked and drained
2 tablespoons chopped
  shallots
2 tablespoons butter or
  margarine
2 tablespoons flour
1½ cups milk
1 cup shredded Swiss cheese
½ teaspoon dill weed
2 tablespoons chopped
  pimiento

Cook peas according to
package directions. While
peas are cooking, sauté
shallots in butter until tender.
Stir in flour and cook until
smooth. Gradually stir in milk
and cook over medium heat,
stirring until thickened and
smooth. Stir in cheese, dill
and pimiento. Add drained
peas. Heat, stirring, until
cheese is melted.

Mashed Swedes

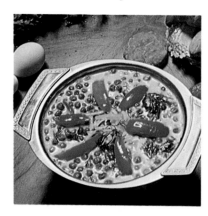

Dilled peas Helsinki

Potato dishes

Norwegian potato balls

Potetboller

4 servings

- 1 cup boiling water
- 1 cup dry instant mashed potatoes
- 8 canned anchovy fillets, finely minced
- 1 tablespoon flour
- 1 tablespoon chopped parsley
- ½ teaspoon salt
- ½ teaspoon dry mustard
- ¼ teaspoon pepper
- ⅛ teaspoon mace
- 1 egg yolk
- 1 cup bread crumbs
  Oil for deep frying

Add boiling water to instant mashed potatoes. Add finely minced anchovy fillets, flour, parsley, salt, mustard, pepper and mace; mix well. Form into walnut-sized balls, coat with beaten egg yolk, then bread crumbs, and deep fry in hot oil (375°) a few at a time until golden brown.

In Scandinavia a potato is not simply a potato – it is a chance to experiment and improvise. Since it is part of the staple diet in the Nordic countries, a wide range of varieties is always available, and it is possible to be served a different potato dish every day for weeks.

Swedish style creamed potatoes

Stuvad potatis

4 servings

- 1½ tablespoons margarine or butter
- 1½ tablespoons flour
- 1¾ cups light cream
- 6 medium boiled potatoes, sliced or diced
- 1 teaspoon salt
- ½ teaspoon white pepper
- 1 tablespoon chopped dill, chives or parsley

In a saucepan, heat margarine, stir in flour; add cream; cook 5 minutes over moderate heat. Stir constantly. Add potatoes, salt and pepper; heat thoroughly. Garnish with chopped herb.

Swedish potatoes

Skånsk potatis

4 servings

- 2 tablespoons shortening
- 6 medium potatoes, diced
- 1 medium onion, chopped
- 1 teaspoon salt
- ½ teaspoon white pepper
- 1¾ cups cream
- 1 tablespoon chopped parsley

In large frying pan, heat shortening, add potatoes and onion; cook on medium heat about 10 minutes or until well browned. Sprinkle with salt and pepper. Gradually add cream, and simmer 10 minutes or until potatoes are tender. Sprinkle with parsley.

Danish fried potato cakes

Raggmunkar

4 servings

- 1 egg
- 1 cup flour
- 2 cups milk
- 1½ teaspoons salt
- 6 medium potatoes, peeled, cut into 1" cubes
- ¼ cup salad oil

In blender jar, combine egg, flour, milk and salt; blend ½ minute. Add a few pieces of potato at a time until all are blended into batter. Heat a thin layer of oil on a griddle or frying pan; use about 1 tablespoon batter for small cakes or 2 to 3 tablespoons for large crepe-type cake, spreading thinly. Fry on both sides until crisp and brown. Serve with a fruit preserve, maple syrup, or plain with meat.

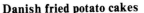
Danish fried potato cakes

Swedish hasselback potatoes

Hasselbackspotatis

4 servings

- 12 *oval-shaped potatoes, peeled*
- 1 *teaspoon salt*
- 3 *tablespoons margarine or butter*
- 4 *tablespoons grated Parmesan cheese*
- 2 *tablespoons bread crumbs*

Cut potatoes into thin slices, but not quite through to the lower edge, so that the slices hold together. Place potatoes, with slices upward, into a well-buttered casserole. Sprinkle with salt and dot with bits of margarine. Bake in a very hot oven (450°) 20 minutes; basting occasionally. Sprinkle with cheese and bread crumbs and bake another 25 minutes without basting.

Finnish stewed potatoes

Muhennetut perunat

4 servings

- 6 *medium potatoes, sliced or diced*
- 2 *cups light cream*
- 1 *teaspoon salt*
- ½ *teaspoon white pepper*
- 1 *tablespoon finely-chopped chives*

Place potatoes in a heavy saucepan; add 1½ cups cream; bring to a boil; reduce heat and simmer over very low heat. Gradually add remaining cream, (just enough to be absorbed by time the potatoes are tender). Season with salt and pepper. Sprinkle with chopped chives.

Danish browned potatoes

Brunede kartofler

4 servings

- 2 *pounds small potatoes, unpeeled*
- ½ *cup sugar*
- 3 *tablespoons margarine or butter*

Boil potatoes in their skins; peel while still hot. In a saucepan, brown sugar and add margarine, stirring constantly. Add potatoes and turn carefully until potatoes are coated on all sides.

Smalandsk potato cakes

Småländska raggmunkar

4 servings

- 2½ *pounds potatoes, peeled, and cut into large cubes*
- 1½ *teaspoons salt*
  Water, if needed
- ½ *cup oil*

Start blender on high speed. Add potato cubes a few at a time until finely chopped. Add salt, and if mixture is very thick add a drop or two of water. Heat large, heavy skillet; cover surface with thin layer of oil. For each cake, pour 2 to 3 tablespoons of potato mixture onto hot pan; spread thinly. Brown well on each side over moderate heat until cakes are very crisp. Drain on paper towels. Serve immediately.

Swedish hasselback potatoes

Smalandsk potato cakes

Skansk mustard sauce

Skånsk senapssås

Makes 1 cup

  1 cup sour cream
  1 tablespoon prepared mustard
  1 teaspoon instant minced
    onion
  1 teaspoon lemon juice
  ¼ teaspoon salt
  ⅛ teaspoon black pepper
  1 tablespoon chopped scallion

Combine all ingredients; blend
well. Serve with fish or egg
dishes.

Danish mustard sauce

Sennepsauce til gravlaks

  Brown sugar
  Prepared mustard
  Finely chopped dill

Mix equal amounts of brown
sugar and mustard together
until smooth. Sprinkle with
chopped dill. Serve with
marinated salmon or baked
ham.

Swedish sauce for salmon

Gravlaxsås

Makes ¾ cup

  7 tablespoons oil
  2 tablespoons vinegar
  2 tablespoons prepared mustard
  1 egg yolk
  1 tablespoon sugar
  ¼ teaspoon salt
  ¼ teaspoon dill weed

Combine all ingredients in small
jar; cover. Shake vigorously
until well blended. Serve over
pickled salmon or fish.

Remoulade sauce

Remouladesås

Makes 1¼ cups

  ½ cup mayonnaise
  ½ cup sour cream
  5 gherkin pickles, chopped
  1 scallion, finely chopped
  1 tablespoon capers
  1 teaspoon chopped chives
  1 teaspoon chopped parsley
    Dash black pepper

Combine all ingredients; blend
well. Serve with fish and
shellfish.

Swedish chive sauce

Gräslökssås

Makes ¾ cup

  ½ cup margarine or butter
  3 egg yolks
  2 tablespoons lemon juice
  ¼ teaspoon salt
  1 tablespoon chopped chives

Heat margarine until bubbly but not brown. Place egg yolks, lemon juice, and salt in blender jar. Blend on low speed. Immediately pour in margarine in a slow stream. Add chives; beat 10 seconds. Serve with fish.

Swedish sauce velouté

Ljus grundsås

Makes 1 cup

  2 tablespoons margarine or butter
  2 tablespoons flour
  1 chicken or beef bouillon cube
  1 cup hot water

Melt margarine in small saucepan over medium heat. Stir in flour until well blended. Dissolve bouillon cube in water; gradually stir into flour mixture. Cook over medium heat, stirring constantly, until thickened and bubbly.

Swedish egg sauce

Äggsås

Makes 1¼ cups

  ¼ cup margarine or butter
  1 tablespoon flour
  1 cup milk
  2 teaspoons prepared mustard
  ½ teaspoon salt
  Dash black pepper
  2 hard cooked eggs, chopped
  2 teaspoons chopped parsley

Melt margarine in small saucepan over medium heat. Stir in flour until well blended. Gradually stir milk into flour mixture until well blended. Stir in mustard, salt and pepper. Cook over medium heat, stirring constantly until thickened and bubbly. Stir in eggs and parsley. Serve with fish.

Swedish horseradish sauce

Pepparrotssås

Makes 1½ cups

  1 recipe sauce velouté, this page
  ½ cup heavy cream
  2–3 tablespoons horseradish

Prepare sauce veloute according to directions. Stir in cream and horseradish. Serve with poached fish or boiled beef.

Danish poached fish

Indkogt fisk

4 servings

- 1 quart water
- 2 teaspoons salt
- 2 tablespoons vinegar
- 3 peppercorns
- 5 whole allspice
- 1 bay leaf
- 2 pounds whole, cleaned fish or fish fillets (cod, haddock, mackerel)
  Dill or parsley

In a large saucepan, combine water, salt, vinegar, peppercorns, allspice, and bay leaf. Bring to a boil and boil for 10 to 15 minutes. Add fish. Cover; simmer 6 to 8 minutes. Remove from heat; allow fish to cool in bouillon. Remove fish from bouillon and garnish with dill or parsley.

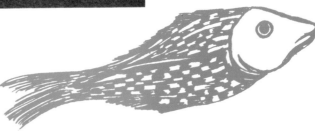

Swedish eel in aspic

Ålaladåb

4 to 6 servings

1½ pounds eel or small trout
1 (12 ounce) package frozen
   cleaned shrimp
   Water
1 teaspoon salt
1 medium onion, sliced
4 peppercorns
2 bay leaves
2 tablespoons vinegar
1 envelope unflavored gelatin
½ cup cold water
2 hard cooked eggs, cut into
   wedges
1 (10 ounce) package frozen
   tiny peas, cooked and cooled
   Parsley or dill

Skin and fillet eel or trout. Place
in saucepan with shrimp; add
water to cover. Add salt, onion,
peppercorns and bay leaves.
Heat until just below boiling;
poach fish and shrimp until just
tender, about 3 to 5 minutes.
Do Not Overcook. Carefully
remove fish and shrimp; strain
liquid, stir in vinegar and
reserve. Soften gelatin in cold
water; stir into hot fish liquid
until dissolved. Arrange shrimp
in bottom of rinsed 1½-quart
ring mold. Cover with
gelatin-fish liquid. Arrange fish
pieces and hard cooked egg
wedges over shrimp, cover with
more gelatin mixture. Arrange
peas over fish pieces; cover with
remaining gelatin mixture. Chill
until set about 2 hours. Turn out
on round platter. Serve cold,
garnished with parsley or dill.

Swedish pickled

Glasmästarsill

4 servings

2 salted schmalz herring,
   filleted and skinned
½ cup vinegar
1 cup water
1 small red or sweet white
   onion, thinly sliced
4 bay leaves
1 tablespoon black pepper
¾ cup sugar
1 carrot, sliced

Cover herring fillets with cold
water; soak overnight in
refrigerator. Drain and rinse;
Cut into 1½″ pieces. Place
in a non-metallic bowl. Combine
remaining ingredients and pour
over herring. Refrigerate at
least 4 hours before serving.
(Will keep for several days.)

Jansson's temptation

Janssons frestelse

4 to 6 servings

3 medium onions, cut in rings
2 tablespoons margarine or
   butter, melted
6 potatoes, peeled and cut into
   ½″ strips
1 (2 ounce) can anchovy fillets
1 cup heavy cream or
   evaporated milk

Sauté onion rings in margarine
until golden brown. In a buttered
2-quart casserole, place alternate
layers of potatoes, onion rings,
and anchovies ending with a
layer of potatoes. Carefully pour
cream over top of potatoes; dot
with margarine. Bake in
moderate oven (350°) 45 to 50
minutes or until potatoes are
tender.

Norwegian fish mold

Fiskepudding

4 to 6 servings

2 (1 pound) packages frozen
   haddock fillets, thawed
2 teaspoons salt
¼ teaspoon black pepper
1 cup milk
1 cup cream or evaporated
   milk
1½ tablespoons cornstarch
1 tablespoon margarine or
   butter
4 tablespoons dry bread crumb

In blender, add fish fillets, salt,
pepper, milk, and cream in
small amounts; blend until
mixture is thoroughly pureed.
Beat in cornstarch. Butter a
2-quart mold; sprinkle with
bread crumbs until completely
covered; remove excess crumbs.
Carefully pour in pureed fish
mixture. Place mold in pan of
hot water. Bake in a moderate
oven (350°) about 1 hour or unt
top of mold is firm to touch.
Unmold carefully on platter and
serve warm.

*No buffet supper in Sweden is
complete without shiny, chilled
eel in aspic (left), pickled
herring (right) and Jansson's
temptation (below)*

Swedish crayfish

Kräftor

4 servings

    6 quarts cold water
    6 tablespoons salt
    1 tablespoon dill seed
    3 bunches fresh dill
   40 crayfish or 4 lobsters

In a very large kettle bring
water, salt, dill seed, and 1 bunch
fresh dill to the boil. Drop
crayfish, 8 to 10 at a time, into
boiling water. Cook 6 to 7
minutes. (Or plunge lobsters into
boiling water; cook 10 minutes
for 2-pound lobsters, 7 minutes
for lobsters less than 2 pounds.)
Add fresh dill with each addition
of crayfish. Remove crayfish
from water; drain. Garnish with
remaining dill. Serve with
toast and melted butter, if
desired.

Danish cod roe

Kogt torskerogn

4 servings

  1¾ pounds cod roe
    2 quarts water
    2 tablespoons salt
    2 tablespoons chopped dill or
       parsley

Carefully wash roe; do not break
membrane. In a large 3-quart
saucepan, heat water with salt
and dill to boiling. Reduce heat
and bring water to a simmer.
Gently put in roe. Simmer until
done about 5 to 10 minutes
depending on size. Carefully
remove roe and serve with lemon
slices.

Swedish chimney sweeps

Sotare

4 servings

    2 pounds fresh trout
    2 tablespoons salad oil
    2 teaspoons salt

Clean, rinse, and dry fish. Brush
with oil and sprinkle with salt.
Shape a shallow pan out of
several sheets of aluminum foil.
Brush pan with oil and place fish
in it. Place over glowing
charcoals and cook until fish
flakes easily when tested with a
fork. (Fish may be broiled in
broiler 4 to 5 minutes or until
done.)

Swedish sauced trout

Stuvad fisk

4 servings

    1 recipe broiled trout
  1½ cups vinegar
    ½ cup sugar
   20 allspice berries
    3 bay leaves
    1 small white or red onion,
       thinly sliced
       Dill or parsley sprigs

Heat vinegar, sugar, allspice,
bay leaves and sliced onion to
boiling point. Remove from
heat and leave to cool. Prepare
trout according to directions for
Swedish chimney sweeps (see
previous recipe). Place fish in
a bowl while still hot. Pour
vinegar mixture over hot fish.

*Fresh trout from icy Swedish
mountain streams is first fried,
and then marinated in vinegar
with herbs.*

Swedish sauced trout

Danish baked stuffed fish

Ovnstegt fyldt fisk

4 servings

 1 medium bluefish or mackerel
 ½ teaspoon salt
 ¼ teaspoon black pepper
 2 tablespoons lemon juice
 1 small onion, finely chopped
 2 tablespoons margarine or
    butter
 ⅓ cup water
 1 cup packaged bread stuffing

Clean fish; wash and dry.
Sprinkle with salt, pepper, and
lemon juice. Sauté onion in
margarine until transparent and
golden brown. Add onions and
water to stuffing mix. Fill cavity
with stuffing. Fasten edges with
wooden toothpicks. Place in
buttered baking dish. Bake in
moderately hot oven (375°)
35 to 40 minutes or until fish
flakes when tested with a fork.

Norwegian stuffed herring

Fylld sild

4 servings

 2 pounds fresh herring, smelts,
    or other small fish
 2 teaspoons salt
 2 tablespoons chopped chives
 2 tablespoons finely chopped
    onions
 ¼ cup dry bread crumbs
 3 tablespoons margarine or
    butter

Clean fish; remove backbones.
Sprinkle with salt. Sandwich
chives and onions between two
fish; coat the fish sandwiches
with bread crumbs. Melt
margarine in a large skillet;
fry fish until golden brown on
both sides.

Swedish smoked fish in foil

Fiskfilé i folie

4 servings

 4 (½ pound each) smoked fish
 4 pieces foil, approximately
    12" square
 4 teaspoons water

Score skin of fish. Place one fish
on each square of foil; sprinkle
each with one teaspoon water.
Bend edges of foil up to make a
close-fitting pan, without
covering top of fish. Place on
cookie sheet. Bake in a very hot
oven (450°) about 3 to 5
minutes, or until heated through.
(The fish should be restored to
a "just smoked" flavor, not
browned or baked.)

Danish fish in foil

Rökt fisk i folie

6 servings

 2 (1 pound) packages frozen
    fish fillets, thawed
 1 teaspoon salt
 ¼ teaspoon black pepper
 2 tablespoons lemon juice
 1 (10½ ounce) can cream of
    shrimp soup
 ¼ cup cream or evaporated
    milk
 1½ cups cooked shrimp, deveined

Arrange fillets on six pieces of
buttered aluminum foil about
12 inches square. Sprinkle with
salt, pepper, and lemon juice.
Combine soup, cream, and
shrimp. Spoon stuffing on half
of fish fillets; fold the other half
over stuffing. Fold foil over
stuffed fillets and fold edges
together to make a pocket.
Place in a large shallow baking
dish. Bake in a moderately hot
oven (375°) 25 to 30 minutes or
until fish flakes when tested with
a fork.

Swedish smoked fish in foil

Danish flounder and spinach casserole

Rödspaette og spinat

4 servings

  1 (1 pound) package frozen
      flounder fillets, thawed
  2 tablespoons flour
  ½ teaspoon salt
  ⅛ teaspoon black pepper
  2 eggs, beaten
  ½ cup dry bread crumbs
  ¼ cup margarine or butter
  1 (9 ounce) package frozen
      creamed spinach
  1 (3 ounce) can sliced
      mushrooms

Separate fish fillets. Dust with flour; sprinkle with salt and pepper. Dip floured fillets in beaten egg, then in bread crumbs. Brown fillets in margarine. Cook spinach according to package directions. Pour spinach in bottom of shallow casserole. Top with fillets and then mushrooms. Heat in a moderate oven (350°) 15 to 20 minutes or until heated thoroughly.

Seafood is an important ingredient in many Scandinavian dishes.

Norwegian fried flounder with onion sauce

Norwegian fried flounder with onion sauce

Stekt flyndre i løk saus

4 servings

  1 (1 pound) package frozen
      flounder fillets, thawed
  4 tablespoons flour
  2 eggs, beaten
  ½ cup bread crumbs
  4 tablespoons margarine or
      butter, melted

Dip fillets in flour, then beaten egg, and finally in bread crumbs. Fry in large skillet in melted margarine until golden brown. Remove from skillet and keep warm.

Onion sauce:

  3 tablespoons margarine or
      butter
  2 medium onions, finely
      chopped
  2 tablespoons flour
  ½ teaspoon salt
  ¼ teaspoon black pepper
  ½ teaspoon sugar
  1½ cups milk
  2 tablespoons chopped green
      pepper (optional)

Melt margarine and sauté onions until transparent; remove from skillet. Stir flour, salt, pepper, and sugar into remaining margarine in skillet; gradually add milk. Cook and stir until sauce thickens. Add onions and cook, stirring constantly, for 2 to 3 minutes. Stir in chopped green pepper if desired. Serve sauce with fried flounder fillets or fried herring (recipe page 49).

Swedish herring balls

Sillbullar

4 to 6 servings

1 (3¼ ounce) can kippered
  herring, drained
4 cold boiled potatoes,
  mashed
½ pound ground beef, cooked
  and drained
1 small onion, chopped
1 tablespoon flour
½ teaspoon salt
⅛ teaspoon black pepper
2 tablespoons milk
4 tablespoons dry bread
  crumbs
3 tablespoons margarine or
  butter

Chop herring. Combine with
potatoes, beef, and onion until
well blended. Add flour, salt, and
pepper. Stir in milk gradually,
using a little more, if necessary,
until mixture is of a consistency
that can be shaped into 1″
balls. Roll balls in bread crumbs.
Melt margarine in large heavy
skillet; brown balls in margarine.
Serve hot.

Norwegian cod

Kokt torsk

4 servings

1½ quarts water
3 tablespoons salt
4 cod steaks, ¾″ thick
¼ pound margarine or butter,
  melted
1 tablespoon chopped parsley
1 tablespoon chopped chives
½ teaspoon salt
⅛ teaspoon black pepper

In a large saucepan, bring water
and salt to a boil. Carefully add
fish steaks. Reduce heat so that
water just simmers; cook 5 to 8
minutes. Remove fish from
water with slotted spoon; keep
warm. Stir together melted
margarine, parsley, chives, salt
and pepper. Heat mixture to the
simmering point. Serve sauce
with cod steaks.

Danish cod fish casserole

Gryderet med torsk

4 servings

1 (1 pound) package frozen
  cod fillets, thawed
1 (2 ounce) can flat anchovies
3 tablespoons bread crumbs
3 tablespoons margarine or
  butter

Separate cod fillets. Drain
anchovies and chop finely;
spread over each fillet. Roll
fillets. Place in a buttered 1½
quart casserole, sprinkle on
bread crumbs; dot with
margarine. Bake in a moderate
oven (350°) 25 to 30 minutes or
until fish flakes when tested with
a fork.

Norwegian fish balls

Fiskeboller

4 to 6 servings

1 (1 pound) package frozen
  cod fillets, thawed
1 teaspoon salt
⅔ cup heavy cream or
  evaporated milk
2 eggs
1 tablespoon cornstarch
1 quart water
2 bouillon cubes

Cut fish into pieces. Place half
of the fish in blender jar.
Combine cream, eggs, and
cornstarch. Pour half of cream
mixture into blender jar. Blend
thoroughly. Empty into small
mixing bowl. Repeat with
remaining fish and cream
mixture. Stir all the blended fish
mixture together. Chill
thoroughly. Pour water into a
large, wide saucepan. Add
bouillon cubes; bring to a boil.
Lower heat so that bouillon is
just simmering. Using two
teaspoons to make balls, drop
fish mixture into bouillon. Cook
for 8 to 10 minutes. Remove
balls with slotted spoon and
keep warm. Serve with
horseradish sauce.

Swedish herring balls

Norwegian tuna fish casserole

Fiskegryte

4 servings

- *1 (13 ounce) can tuna fish, drained*
- *1 (1 pound) package frozen cottage potato fries, thawed*
- *1 (15 ounce) can tomato sauce*
- *1 (3½ ounce) can french fried onions*
- *1 teaspoon Worcestershire sauce*
- *1 tablespoon chopped parsley*

Flake tuna fish. Arrange alternate layers of tuna fish, potatoes, tomato sauce and onions in a buttered 7″ × 11″ × 2″ baking dish. Sprinkle each tomato sauce layer with Worcestershire sauce and parsley. (Top layer should be onions.) Bake in a moderate oven (350°) 30 to 35 minutes or until tomato sauce bubbles.

Swedish fried herring

Stekt färsk sill

4 servings

- *2 pounds small herrings or smelts*
- *2 teaspoons salt*
- *4 tablespoons rye flour or dry bread crumbs*
- *3 tablespoons margarine or butter*
- *1 recipe onion sauce, page 29*

Clean fish; remove backbones. Wash thoroughly and drain. Add salt to the rye flour or bread crumbs. Roll fish in flour or bread crumbs until well coated. Melt margarine in a large skillet and fry the fish about 3 to 4 minutes on each side. Serve with onion sauce

Norwegian baked fish fillets

Ovnsstekt fiskefilet

3 to 4 servings

- *1 (1 pound) package frozen fish fillets (haddock or cod)*
- *1 tablespoon lemon juice*
- *1 egg, slightly beaten*
- *¼ cup bread crumbs*
- *2 tablespoons margarine or butter*
- *1 lemon, sliced*

Thaw fish fillets; place in well-buttered 7″ × 11″ × 2″ baking dish. Sprinkle with lemon juice; pour beaten egg over fillets. Top with bread crumbs and bits of margarine. Bake in moderate oven (350°) about 30 to 40 minutes or until fish flakes when tested with a fork. Garnish with lemon slices.

Swedish fried flounder fillets

Strömmingsflundror

4 servings

- *1 (1 pound) package frozen flounder fillets, thawed*
- *4 tablespoons dry bread crumbs*
- *2 medium onions, thinly sliced*
- *3 tablespoons margarine or butter, melted*
- *½ cup cream*

Coat fish fillets with breadcrumbs. In a large skillet, sauté onions in melted margarine until transparent and golden brown. Remove onions from pan; keep warm. In the same skillet, fry fillets over moderate heat until golden brown, about 4 minutes on each side. Place fillets on platter; cover with cooked onions. Pour cream into skillet and heat almost to boil. Pour over fish fillets and onions. Serve immediately.

Not every fresh herring is soaked and pickled in a careful blend of savory sauces. Some still find their way into the frying pan, to come out a crisp golden brown.

Swedish fried herring

Swedish herring a l'Opera Cellar

Strömming à la Opris

4 servings

   2 pounds frozen smelts, thawed
   2 egg yolks
   1 cup evaporated milk
   ⅓ cup rye flour
   2 teaspoons salt
   3 tablespoons margarine or
      butter

Clean smelts; remove backbones.
Blend egg yolks and milk. Add
smelts and let stand for a
half-hour. Carefully remove
smelts so that as much of the
milk as possible remains on fish.
Quickly dip in flour mixed with
salt, turning until coated. Melt
margarine in large skillet. Fry
smelts until medium brown,
about 3 to 4 minutes on each
side.

*Swedish herring a l'Opera Cellar.
Fried seafood finds its perfect
accompaniment in ice-cold beer
and thinly sliced dark rye bread.*

In the enjoyable book by Selma Lagerlöf, that tells the story of the fantastic travels of young Nils Holgersson, the little Swedish boy rides through the country on the back of a wild goose. Each year the geese return in their V-formation against the blue sky, and their long cry echoes in the stillness of the Swedish forest. They are on their way to Lapland in the far north. Other animals, which have disappeared from almost all the rest of Europe, still live in the woods of Sweden, Norway and Finland. The bear and the elk are two examples. These animals are protected by law, and each year only a carefully restricted number can be killed. In Swedish and Finnish restaurants a leg of bear sometimes appears on the menu. It is a dark brown, slightly tough meat with an adventurous and wild flavor. Vast herds of reindeer roam the frozen tundra of the far north, and reindeer is a Scandinavian delicacy. Cold reindeer served with a compote of arctic berries belongs in any festive smörgåsbord. Reindeer tongue in jelly with sour cream is among the most delicious snacks of famous gourmet restaurants. Another gourmet dish is the unique pâté which the chef can make from the snow grouse of Lapland.

Swedish chicken

Kokt höns

6 servings

- ¼ cup margarine or butter
- 6 boned chicken breasts
- ½ cup dry white wine
- 2 tablespoons gin
- 1 teaspoon dill weed
- ½ teaspoon powdered thyme
- ½ teaspoon salt

Melt margarine in large skillet over medium heat. Brown chicken in margarine. Add wine, gin, dill, thyme and salt. Cover. Simmer about 20 minutes or until chicken is tender.

Danish fried chicken

Stegt kylling

4 servings

- 1 (3½ to 4 pound) roasting chicken
- 1 bunch parsley
  Salt and pepper
- ½ cup butter or margarine
  About 2 cups water or chicken stock

Wash and dry chicken. Rinse parsley and place in cavity of chicken. Season. Melt butter in Dutch oven. Brown chicken all over. Add ½ cup water or stock, cover and cook over medium heat until liquid evaporates. Continue turning chicken and adding liquid, ½ cup at a time for about 45 minutes or until chicken is tender. If crisper skin is desired, cut chicken in half and place under broiler for a few minutes. Serve with the parsley, browned potatoes, cucumber salad and currant jelly.

Swedish roast chicken

Stekt kyckling

6 servings

- 4 tablespoons margarine or butter
- 1 onion, chopped
- 1 cup chopped celery
- ½ cup chopped dried apricots
- 1 teaspoon salt
- ½ teaspoon thyme
- ¼ teaspoon sage
- 2 chicken bouillon cubes
- ⅓ cup water
- 6 slices (3 cups) white bread, cubed
- 1 (5 pound) roasting chicken

Melt margarine in large skillet; sauté onion and celery until onion is transparent. Stir in apricots, salt, thyme, sage, bouillon cubes and water. Heat to boiling, crushing bouillon cube. Remove from heat. Add bread cubes; toss lightly until evenly moistened. Wash chicken and pat dry. Stuff neck and body cavities lightly with stuffing. Skewer openings closed. Place chicken on rack in shallow roasting pan. Roast in a moderately hot oven (375°) about 2½ hours or until drumstick moves easily at joint. Thicken pan drippings if desired.

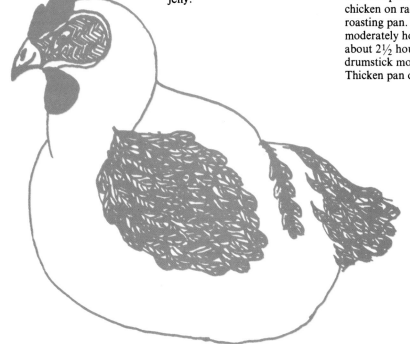

Samsoe chicken

Kylling med Samsø ost

4 servings

- 2 *large chicken breasts cut in half, or 4 legs*
- 1 *leek*
- 1 *carrot*
- 1 *celery stalk*
   Water
   Salt
- 3 *tablespoons butter*
- 3 *tablespoons flour*
- ½ *pound cooked ham, cut in strips*
- 1 *medium red pepper, cut in strips and blanched*
- ½ *pound Samsoe cheese, sliced*
   Paprika

Place chicken and vegetables in a pot. Cover with water, add a dash of salt and boil about 25 minutes until tender. Retain stock. Melt butter; add flour and stir until blended. Remove from heat and slowly add 1½ cups chicken stock. Return to heat and stir constantly over low heat until thickened. Add ham and red pepper to sauce. Place drained chicken in oven-proof serving dish and cover with sauce. Layer cheese slices over top and sprinkle lightly with paprika. Bake at 350° for about 5 minutes until cheese is melted and lightly browned.

Finnish rabbit fricassee

Jänispaisti

4 servings

- 6 *slices bacon, diced*
- 1 *(2½ pound) package frozen rabbit, thawed*
- 2 *chicken bouillon cubes*
- 1 *cup hot water*
- 2 *tablespoons flour*
- ½ *teaspoon salt*
- 1 *cup heavy cream*
- 1 *tablespoon red currant jelly*

In large skillet, fry bacon until crisp; remove. Drain off fat; return ¼ cup fat to skillet. Brown rabbit on both sides. Dissolve bouillon cubes in water; pour over rabbit. Cover. Cook over medium heat until rabbit is tender, about 45 minutes. Remove rabbit; keep warm. Stir flour and salt into cream. Gradually stir cream into pan liquid. Cook, stirring constantly, until thickened. Stir in jelly until melted. Add bacon. Pour gravy over rabbit.

Goose fat

Gåsfett

Place excess fat from cavity of goose in a small saucepan. Cover with water. Bring to a boil; continue to boil until fat melts. Remove from heat; strain through cheesecloth into small bowl. When fat solidifies, pour off water. Use for frying or bread baking.

Norwegian black pot

Sort gryte

6 servings

- 1 *(10½ ounce) can cream of mushroom soup*
- 1 *cup milk*
- ½ *teaspoon salt*
- ½ *teaspoon black pepper*
- 2 *cups cooked, diced chicken*
- 1 *cup cooked, diced ham*
- 1 *(10 ounce) package frozen peas*
- 2 *leeks, cooked and cut into ½" pieces*
- 4 *tomatoes, peeled and quartered*
- ¼ *cup Madeira wine*

In a large saucepan, combine soup, milk, salt and pepper; blend well. Heat. Stir in chicken, ham, peas, leeks and tomatoes. Cook, stirring occasionally, until heated about 10 minutes. Stir in wine. Serve with cornbread, if desired.

Denmark is a paradise for the lean and streamlined Danish hog. It is said that in this friendly, tidy land there are twice as many hogs as people. The Danes are naturally fond of their pork, but its fame has spread far beyond Denmark's borders. The English especially love delicious Danish pork chops, ham and Danish bacon, and consequently the Danes often find less of their own pork in stores than they would like, since most of it is exported. Meat is scarcer than fish throughout most of Scandinavia. And this is nowhere truer than in the remote mountains of Norway, where there is no land suitable for grazing cattle and beef has become a luxury item.
It is partly because of the need to be economical with meat that the Scandinavians are so good at making meatballs. Meatballs are nowhere more delicious than in these northern countries: delicate, soft and tender, carefully seasoned so that the flavor of the meat can be tasted in its own right when it is fried, and served with an exquisite cream sauce. No Swedish or Finnish smörgåsbord is complete without a pot of full-flavored brown meatballs accompanied by crisp cabbage.

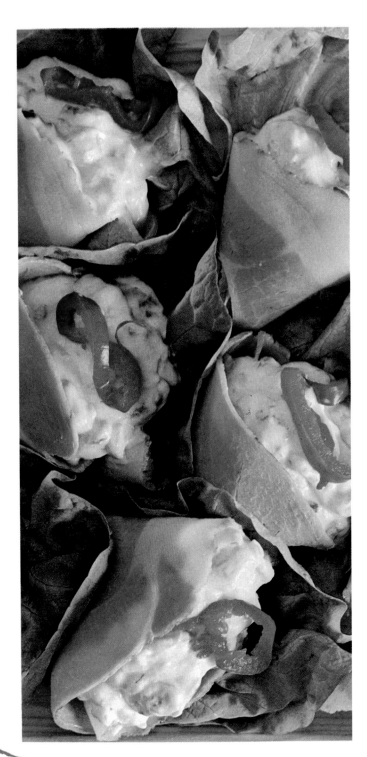

Swedish ham rolls

Fyllda skinkrulader

4 servings

- 1 cup cooked green peas
- 1 apple, diced
- 1 teaspoon lemon juice
- 2 hard cooked eggs, chopped
- 1 teaspoon capers, chopped
- ½ cup heavy cream, whipped
- ½ cup mayonnaise
- 1 tablespoon grated horseradish
- 1 (10 ounce) package frozen asparagus spears, cooked and chilled
- 12 slices boiled ham, about ¾ pound

Combine peas, apple, lemon juice, eggs and capers; chill. In another bowl, blend cream, mayonnaise, and horseradish; chill. Stir ½ cup of the cream dressing into the peas and apple mixture. Place about ¼ cup of the mixture on half of the ham slices and roll to form logs. Place asparagus on remaining ham slices and roll into logs. Serve ham rolls with remaining dressing. Garnish with strips of pimento, if desired.

Ham and asparagus, a classic combination of delicate flavors, with sweet cream, a characteristic Swedish touch.

Finnish roast fresh ham

Kinkku

4 servings

½ *fresh ham*
1 *teaspoon salt*
¼ *teaspoon pepper*
1 *medium tart apple, sliced*
1 *medium onion, chopped*
10 *cooked prunes, pitted*
1 *tablespoon chopped parsley*
1 *bouillon cube*
1 *cup boiling water*

Score top of ham in diamond pattern. Cut large pocket in meat directly under the top, cutting from the side. Sprinkle meat and inside of pocket with salt and pepper. Combine apple, onion, prunes, and parsley; fill cavity. Fasten opening with wooden picks or skewers. Place ham in roasting pan and roast in moderate oven (350°) allowing 30 to 35 minutes per pound. Remove meat and keep warm. Pour off excess fat. Stir bouillon and boiling water into pan and blend with pan juices. Serve gravy with slices of meat.

Danish baked ham and eggs

Skinke med spejlag

6 servings

½ *pound Havarti cheese, coarsely shredded*
6 *slices Danish ham*
6 *eggs*
½ *cup milk*
1½ *teaspoons powdered mustard*
¾ *teaspoon salt*
  Dash of pepper
3 *tablespoons butter, melted*

Sprinkle grated cheese over the bottom of a well-buttered baking dish (11¼″ x 7¼″). Break eggs over cheese. Top each egg with slice of ham. Combine milk, mustard, salt, pepper, butter and pour over eggs and ham. Bake at 350° for 15 minutes, or until eggs are set.

Danish ham and potato dinner

Skinke a la' viksemad

4 servings

1 *(16 ounce) can Danish Picnic or ham, chilled and cubed*
2 *hard boiled eggs, quartered*
4 *medium potatoes, peeled and cubed*
3 *tablespoons butter*
  Parsley

Melt butter in large skillet. Fry potatoes slowly for 15 to 20 minutes. Add ham and fry quickly to brown. Turn into heated serving dish. Garnish with eggs and parsley.

Swedish meat balls

Köttbullar

4 servings

Meat mixture:
1 *pound ground beef*
¼ *pound ground pork*
½ *cup fine dry bread crumbs*
1 *cup milk*
½ *teaspoon salt*
¼ *teaspoon white pepper*
1 *egg*
2 *tablespoons finely chopped onion*

Gravy:
2 *tablespoons margarine or butter*
1 *cup half-and-half or beef stock*
1 *tablespoon cornstarch*
2 *tablespoons cold water*

Combine meat mixture ingredients; beat with fork. Shape mixture into 8 large or 40 to 50 small meat balls. Heat margarine in large skillet over moderate heat. Brown meat balls on one side about 2 minutes; turn and brown other side. Reduce heat to low and cover pan; simmer about 15 minutes for large meat balls, 8 minutes for small. Remove meat balls; pour off fat. Add half-and-half or beef stock. Blend cornstarch and water; add to pan. Stir over moderate heat until mixture comes to a boil; taste and if necessary, add salt and pepper. Serve gravy with meat balls.

Baked ham and eggs (left) and Danish ham and potato dinner (right).

Swedish frosted meat loaf

Köttfärs

4 to 6 servings

- *1 recipe meat mixture page 54*
- *2 cups mashed potatoes*
  Beef stock or hot water
- *2 tablespoons cold water*
- *1 tablespoon cornstarch*

Press meat mixture into a greased 9″ × 5″ × 3″ loaf pan. Bake in moderate oven (350°) for 1 hour. Pour off any cooking juices; measure and save. Let loaf cool in pan about 15 minutes. Turn loaf out of pan onto oven-proof platter or pan. Frost completely with mashed potatoes. Place in hot oven (450°) until edges of potatoes are golden brown, about 10 to 15 minutes. Measure reserved juices and add beef stock or water to make 1 cup. Blend cornstarch and water; add to juices. Cook over moderate heat, stirring constantly, until gravy comes to a boil. Taste; season with salt and pepper, if needed.

Swedish meat dumplings

Frikadeller

4 servings

- *2 tablespoons fine dry bread crumbs*
- *½ cup half-and-half*
- *½ pound ground veal*
- *½ pound ground pork*
- *2 egg yolks*
- *½ teaspoon salt*
  Dash ground white pepper
- *4 bouillon cubes*
- *4 cups boiling water*

Soak bread crumbs in half-and-half. Combine veal, pork, crumb mixture, egg yolks, salt and pepper; beat with fork. Using teaspoons, shape into small meat balls. In large saucepan, dissolve bouillon cubes into boiling water; add meat balls a few at a time. Simmer over moderate heat about 5 minutes. Remove with slotted spoon. Drain on paper towels; keep warm. Serve with dill, lemon, tomato or caper sauce if desired.

Swedish meat cakes garni

Pannbiff

4 servings

- *1 pound ground beef*
- *2 tablespoons margarine or butter*
- *½ teaspoon salt*
  Dash ground white pepper
- *4 large hamburger buns, toasted*
- *4 tablespoons mayonnaise*
- *4 tablespoons catsup*
- *16 slices dill pickle*
- *16 very thin slices tomato*
- *4 slices sweet Bermuda onion*
- *4 leaves lettuce*
  Radish roses or parsley sprigs, if desired

Shape beef into four large round patties. In large skillet, melt margarine and cook patties over moderate heat until browned on both sides and center is cooked to desired degree of doneness. Sprinkle with salt and pepper. Spread each bun with 1 tablespoon mayonnaise, place pattie on bun; spread 1 tablespoon catsup on each pattie. Top each pattie with 4 slices dill pickle, 4 slices tomato, 1 slice Bermuda onion and 1 lettuce leaf. Serve garnished with radish roses and parsley sprigs, if desired.

Danish meat balls

Frikadeller

10 Servings

 1 pound finely ground pork
 1 pound finely ground veal
 ½ cup flour
 5 eggs
 1½ pints milk
 2 teaspoons salt
 ½ teaspoon white pepper
 1 large onion, finely grated
    Butter for frying

Mix meat with salt, pepper and onion juice. Add flour, eggs and milk little by little, and mix thoroughly. Make into balls about 3″ in diameter. Brown in butter. Turn down heat and fry slowly for about 5 minutes, uncovered. Serve with red cabbage or creamed cauliflower.

Swedish hash

Pytt i panna

4 servings

 2 medium onions, chopped
 2 tablespoons margarine or butter
 2 cups diced, cooked beef or pork
 4–5 medium potatoes cooked, peeled and diced
 1 teaspoon salt
 ¼ teaspoon black pepper
 4 fried eggs
 1 tablespoon chopped parsley

In a large heavy skillet, sauté onions in margarine until golden and transparent. Add diced meat, potatoes, salt and pepper. Cook until mixture is lightly browned. Top each serving with a fried egg; sprinkle with parsley.

Swedish collops

Kalops

6 servings

 3 pounds beef for stew
 1 teaspoon salt
 ¼ teaspoon black pepper
 ¼ cup flour
 3 tablespoons salad oil
 2 medium onions, chopped
 2 bay leaves
 1 (1 pound) can whole cranberry sauce

Sprinkle meat with salt and pepper. Dredge meat with flour. Heat oil in Dutch oven; brown meat in oil on all sides. Add onions, bay leaves and cranberry sauce; stir. Cover. Cook over medium heat, stirring occasionally, until meat is tender about 1½ hours.

Swedish pork chops

Fläskkotletter

4 servings

 1 teaspoon salt
 ½ teaspoon black pepper
 ½ teaspoon ground ginger
 2 tablespoons flour
 4 (½″ thick) loin pork chops
 2 tablespoons oil

Mix salt, pepper, ginger, and flour. Dust chops with mixture. In a heavy skillet, brown chops lightly on both sides in hot oil. Lower heat and cook until done, about 20 minutes.

According to legend, dishes such as Swedish hash and collops (photos below) originated on small ships, where the cooks had few means available and had to do their utmost to serve a nourishing daily meal.

Swedish hash

Swedish collops

Swedish loin of pork

Fläskkarré

4 to 6 servings

- 3 pounds loin of pork
- 10 prunes
- 1¼ cups water
- 1 teaspoon salt
- ¼ teaspoon black pepper
- ½ teaspoon ginger
- 2 tablespoons flour

With a sharp knife, make an opening the length of the roast. Cover prunes with water; bring to a boil. Cool. Reserve liquid. Remove prune pits. Rub opening in meat with salt, pepper, and ginger. Insert cooked prunes in opening; secure opening with skewers. Place meat in open roasting pan. Roast in a moderate oven (350°) about 1 hour and 30 to 45 minutes. Remove meat. Pour off all but 3 tablespoons pan drippings. Stir in flour. Slowly add 1¼ cups liquid from prunes. Stir over low heat until thickened and smooth. Serve gravy with sliced pork.

Finnish lamb steaks

Lampaanpaisti

4 servings

- 2 tablespoons salad oil
- 1 clove garlic, minced
- 1 teaspoon crushed rosemary
- 1 teaspoon salt
- ¼ teaspoon black pepper
- 4 (½" thick) lamb steaks

Combine oil, garlic, rosemary, salt and pepper; rub on both sides of lamb steaks. Let lamb steaks stand at least 3 hours. Broil, 3 inches from heat, until brown on one side, about 8 minutes; turn and broil same time on other side.

Swedish pot roast

Slottsstek

6 servings

- 3½–4 pounds rump beef roast
- 1 teaspoon salt
- ¼ teaspoon black pepper
- 2 tablespoons oil
- 1¼ cups beef bouillon
- 2 medium onions, chopped
- 4 anchovy fillets, chopped
- 1 bay leaf
- 5 peppercorns
- 8 allspice berries
- 2 tablespoons vinegar
- 1 tablespoon molasses
- ½ cup heavy cream
- 2 tablespoons flour

Rub beef with salt and pepper. In a heavy, large saucepan, brown beef on all sides in oil. Add bouillon, onion, anchovies, bay leaf, peppercorns, allspice, vinegar, and molasses. Cover and cook over low heat about 2 hours, or until meat is tender. Remove meat and strain pot liquid. Stir flour and cream into liquid. Cook, stirring constantly, until thickened. Serve gravy with sliced pot roast.

Swedish roast pork

Ugnstekt kotlettrad

4 servings

1½ teaspoons powdered ginger
 1 teaspoon salt
 ¼ teaspoon black pepper
 ½ teaspoon dried sage
 3 pounds pork rib roast

Combine ginger, salt, pepper
and sage; rub into pork. Place
pork in shallow roasting pan.
Bake in a moderate oven (350°)
until meat is tender about 1½
hours.

Swedish roast fresh ham

Skinkstek

4 to 6 servings

 ½ fresh ham
 1 teaspoon salt
 ½ teaspoon black pepper
 1 teaspoon ground ginger
 1 teaspoon rosemary
 1 beef bouillon cube
1¼ cups boiling water

Score top of ham in diamond
pattern. Rub ham with salt,
pepper, ginger, and rosemary.
Place ham on rack in roasting
pan. Roast in a moderate oven
(350°) about 2 hours, allowing
30 to 35 minutes per pound.
Remove all but 2 tablespoons of
pan juices. Add bouillon cube
dissolved in boiling water. Stir
to mix with meat juices. Serve
gravy with sliced roast.

Danish loin of pork

Flaeskesteg med rødkål

4 to 6 servings

 3 pounds loin of pork with
    rind on
 3 tablespoons flour
    Salt and Pepper

Score pork rind all over ½"
apart. Season and roast 1½
hours in a 375° oven. After ½
hour, add 1 cup water. Add 1
cup water every 20 minutes.
Roast is cooked when juice
does not run red. Remove
meat and slice. Pour off liquid,
returning 3 tablespoons to
pan. Stir in flour. Skim fat
from remaining liquid and
slowly add 1½ cups to gravy,
stirring over low heat until
thickened and smooth. Serve
with sugar browned potatoes,
red cabbage and cooked
prunes. Pass the gravy
separately.

Danish beef and ham birds

Benlöse fugle

6 servings

 6 (½" thick) slices round
    steak
 1 (4-ounce) package Canadia
    bacon
 6 tablespoons flour
 ½ teaspoon salt
    Dash black pepper
 2 tablespoons salad oil
 1 medium onion, chopped
 2 cups beef bouillon
 ⅓ cup water

Pound beef slices until slightly
flattened. Place bacon on beef
slices; roll up and secure with
wooden toothpicks. Combine
flour, salt and pepper. Dredge
meat rolls with flour; save flour
Heat oil in large heavy skillet.
Brown meat on all sides in oil.
Add onion; cook until
transparent. Stir in bouillon
Cover. Simmer 1½ hours or unt
meat is tender. Remove meat;
keep warm. Mix remaining flou
with water; add to pan liquids.
Cook stirring constantly until
thickened. Serve gravy over
meat.

Swedish roast pork

Swedish veal timbale

Kalvtimbal

6 servings

- 1 cup half-and-half
- 2 eggs, separated
- 2 tablespoons flour
- ¾ pound ground veal
- 3 tablespoons softened margarine or butter
- 1 teaspoon salt
- ¼ teaspoon ground white pepper
- 3 tablespoons fine dry bread crumbs

Combine half-and-half and egg yolks; stir in flour. Add mixture to veal with 2 tablespoons of the margarine, salt and pepper; beat well with fork. Beat egg whites until stiff; fold into meat mixture. Use remaining margarine to grease a 1½-quart casserole; sprinkle with bread crumbs, coating bottom and sides. Shake off excess; reserve. Turn meat mixture into casserole; sprinkle with reserved crumbs. Cover with lid or aluminum foil. Place in large baking pan filled to a depth of 1″ with boiling water. Bake in hot oven (400°) for 1 hour or until knife inserted near center comes out clean. Let stand 5 minutes; turn out onto warm serving platter.

Dill (shown here in Finnish dill meat) is an age-old Scandinavian herb. Its name comes from the Anglo-Saxon 'dillan,' meaning 'to fall asleep.' In olden times dill extract was taken as a harmless sleeping potion, and according to an ancient popular belief the bride who put a twig of dill in her shoe would be assured of a mild-tempered husband.

Finnish dill meat

Tilliliha

6 servings

- 3 pounds boneless Veal, cut into 1½″ pieces
- 3½ cups water
- 2 teaspoons salt
- 1 teaspoon dill weed
- 10 peppercorns, crushed
- 1 bay leaf
- ½ cup flour
- ¼ cup dry white wine
  Fresh dill or parsley, optional

Place meat in Dutch oven. Add 3 cups of water, salt, dill, peppercorns, and bay leaf. Bring just to a boil; reduce heat. Cover; simmer 1½ hours or until meat is tender. Mix flour and remaining water; stir into meat. Add wine. Continue to cook, stirring constantly until thickened about 3 to 5 minutes. Garnish with chopped dill or parsley.

Swedish veal rollettes

Kalvkyckling

8 servings

- 8 slices ham 6″ × 4″ × ⅛″
- 8 thin veal cutlets, ⅛″ thick
- 4 tablespoons margarine or butter
- ½ cup aquavit or dry white wine
- 1 (8 ounce) package processed Swiss cheese, shredded

Place ham slices on veal; roll up and secure with wooden toothpicks. Melt margarine in large heavy skillet over medium heat. Brown meat on all sides in margarine. Add aquavit. Cover. Cook over medium heat until meat is tender about 8 to 10 minutes. Remove; keep warm. Add cheese. Cook over low heat, stirring constantly, until cheese is melted. Serve sauce over veal rolls.

Swedish sausage casserole

Korvgryta

4 servings

- 1 pound sausage meat
- 2 medium onions, sliced
- 2 apples, sliced
- 4–5 medium potatoes, cooked and sliced

Make 8 patties of sausage meat. Cook in a heavy skillet until lightly browned. Remove and keep warm. Pour off all but 2 tablespoons of drippings. Cook onions in drippings until golden brown and transparent. Add apple slices; cook until tender. In a 2-quart buttered casserole, arrange layers of potatoes, sausage and onion-apple mixture. Bake in a moderate oven (350°) 30 to 35 minutes, or until thoroughly heated.

Finnish lamb stew

Lammasmuhennos

6 servings

3 pounds boneless lamb, cubed
6 potatoes, sliced
4 carrots, cut into 1" pieces
2 leeks, cut into ½" pieces
1 medium onion, sliced
1 cup shredded cabbage
1 teaspoon salt
¼ teaspoon black pepper
3 cups water
1 tablespoon chopped parsley

Place alternate layers of meat
and vegetables in large Dutch
oven. Sprinkle each layer with
salt and pepper. Add water.
Bring to a boil; reduce heat.
Cover. Simmer 1½ hours or
until meat is tender. Sprinkle
with parsley before serving.

*Tender lamb from southern Fin-
land is unrivalled in quality, and
it is one of Finland's favorite
national dishes.*

Norwegian lamb and cabbage stew

Fårikål

6 servings

2 tablespoons salad oil
3 pounds lamb with bone, cut
   into 2" pieces
1 (2 pound) head of cabbage
2 teaspoons salt
2 beef bouillon cubes
2 cups hot water
1 bay leaf
   Chopped parsley

Heat oil in Dutch oven. Brown meat in oil until well browned; remove meat; discard drippings. Wash and trim cabbage; separate into leaves. Place alternate layers of cabbage and meat in Dutch oven. Sprinkle each layer with salt. Add bouillon cubes, water, and bay leaf. Bring to a boil; reduce heat. Cover. Simmer about 1½ hours or until meat is tender. Remove bay leaf. Sprinkle with parsley before serving.

Cabbage and lamb go together naturally, and the two straight-forward flavors complement each other to perfection.

Norwegian crown of lamb

Stekt lammsaddel

6 servings

- 1 (5–6 pound) crown roast of lamb
- 1 tablespoon lemon juice
- 1 tablespoon salad oil
- 2 pounds ground lamb
- 1 clove garlic, minced
- 1 tablespoon chopped parsley
- 1 teaspoon grated lemon rind
- 1 teaspoon salt
- ¼ teaspoon black pepper

Have the bones of the roast "Frenched" that is remove tails from the end bones leaving bones bare. Rub outside of crown with lemon juice and then oil. Combine ground lamb, garlic, parsley, lemon rind, salt and pepper. Place meat mixture inside crown. Pat down firmly and round top. Place on a rack in roasting pan. Bake in a moderate oven (350°) about 1½ hours or to desired degree of doneness. Turn off heat and leave in oven 10 minutes. Place crown on serving plate. Put paper frills on rib bones, if desired. Carve like a pie.

Cabbage pudding

Kålpudding

4 servings

- 1 (1½ pound) head cabbage
- ½ pound ground beef
- ½ pound ground pork
- 1 tablespoon margarine or butter
- ½ teaspoon salt
- ⅛ teaspoon black pepper
- 1 cup mashed potatoes

Remove core and chop cabbage into large pieces. Cook cabbage in boiling salted water only until cabbage wilts. Drain. Cook beef and pork in melted margarine. Combine cooked meat, salt, pepper, and potatoes. Arrange alternate layers of cabbage and meat and potato mixture in a 2-quart casserole. Cover. Bake in a moderate oven (350°) 45 to 50 minutes.

Swedish kidney hash

Hökarpanna

4 servings

- 1 pound beef kidneys
- 4 tablespoons margarine or butter
- 1 pound boneless pork, slivered
- 2 onions, thinly sliced
- 6 medium potatoes, peeled and thinly sliced
- 1 teaspoon salt
- ¼ teaspoon black pepper
- 1 (12 ounce) bottle beer or ale or
- 1½ cups beef bouillon

Remove fat and white veins from kidney; wash; dry with paper towel. Slice kidneys thinly. Melt margarine in large skillet; brown pork and kidneys in margarine. Add onions; cook until transparent. Add potatoes, salt and pepper. Stir in beer. Cook over medium heat, stirring occasionally, until meat is cooked, about 45 minutes.

Danish ground liver steak

Leverböf

4 to 6 servings

- ¾ pound beef liver, cut into pieces
- 5 medium potatoes, peeled and cubed
- 1 teaspoon salt
- ¼ teaspoon black pepper
- 3 tablespoons margarine or butter
- 2 medium onions, thinly sliced
- 1 cup heavy cream

Using grinder or blender, finely chop liver and potatoes together. Add salt and pepper; mix well. Melt margarine in large skillet. Spoon liver-potato mixture into skillet to make 4 to 6 "steaks". Brown on one side about 3 minutes. Place a slice of onion on each "steak". Turn and brown on onion side for 2 to 3 minutes. Carefully remove "steaks" and keep warm. Pour cream into pan and heat to simmering point, stirring to blend with pan juices. Serve with liver "steaks".

A typical example of Danish resource-fulness – transforming ground liver into 'steaks,' and a delicacy even without the usual cream sauce.

Swedish boiled beef

Pepparrotskött

4 servings

2½–3 pounds beef chuck with
   bone
1 quart water
2 teaspoons salt
1 onion, peeled and quartered
2 carrots, cut into 1" slices
1 small yellow turnip, diced
2 stalks celery, cut into 1"
   slices
1 tablespoon margarine or
   butter
2 tablespoons flour
1 bouillon cube
1 cup milk
2–3 teaspoons grated
   horseradish

Place meat in large, heavy
saucepan; cover with water. Add
salt and onion. Bring to a boil;
reduce heat and simmer about
1 hour. Add carrots, turnip, and
celery. Continue to cook until
meat and vegetables are tender,
about 45 minutes. Remove meat
and vegetables and keep warm.
Skim off excess fat. Measure
1 cup cooking liquid. Melt
margarine; stir in flour; add
cooking liquid and bouillon
cube. Gradually add milk and
horseradish. Bring mixture to
boiling point and cook 2
minutes, stirring constantly.
Serve sauce with sliced beef and
vegetables.

Norwegian sailor's stew

Sjömansbiff

4 servings

1½ pounds round steak, cut into
   8 thin slices
3 tablespoons margarine or
   butter
3 medium onions, sliced
8 medium potatoes, sliced
1 teaspoon salt
⅛ teaspoon black pepper
1 pint light ale

Brown steak slices in hot
margarine; remove and keep
warm. Saute onions in remaining
margarine until transparent and
lightly browned; sprinkle with
salt and pepper. Place alternate
layers of meat, onions, and
potatoes in a heavy saucepan.
Pour the pan drippings from
meat and onions over layers.
Add ale. Cover and simmer
gently until potatoes are tender
about 1½ hours.

Swedish beef a la Lindström

Biff à la Lindström

4 servings

1 pound ground beef
1 cup mashed potatoes
1 egg
1 teaspoon salt
¼ teaspoon pepper
½ cup chopped pickled beets
2 tablespoons finely chopped
   onion
2 tablespoons capers, chopped
3 tablespoons margarine or
   butter

Mix together ground beef,
mashed potatoes, egg, salt,
pepper, beets, onion, and capers.
Shape into eight patties. Melt
margarine in a large skillet;
brown patties on each side for
4 to 5 minutes.

Norwegian steak and onions

Biff med lök

4 servings

2 medium onions, sliced
2 tablespoons margarine or
   butter
1½ pounds round steak, cut into
   ½" slices
1 teaspoon salt
¼ teaspoon black pepper

In a large, heavy skillet, cook
onions in margarine until lightly
browned. Remove from pan and
keep warm. Brown steak slices
on each side about 3 minutes,
adding additional margarine if
necessary. Sprinkle with salt and
pepper. Remove steak to serving
dish; top with onions. Pour pan
juices over steak and onions.

Norwegian steak and onions

Desserts

Swedish dried fruit cream

Kräm på torkad frukt

4 to 6 servings

    1 *(12 ounce) package mixed*
        dried fruit
    4 *cups water*
    2 *tablespoons sugar*
  ½ *teaspoon ground mace*
    2 *tablespoons cornstarch*
    3 *tablespoons water*

Simmer fruit in water until
tender, about 15 minutes. Stir in
sugar and mace. Mix cornstarch
with cold water; add to fruit
mixture. Cook over medium
heat, stirring constantly, until
thickened. Stir carefully to avoid
breaking up fruit. Chill. Serve
cold plain, with cream or with
soft or baked custard.

*Because canned fruit has become
so convenient, the full, rich flavor
of dried fruit tends to be for-
gotten. But on distant and iso-
lated farms in Scandinavia,
apples, plums and pears that have
ripened during the summer are
dried and used in preparing delicious sweet dishes throughout the
long winter.*

Swedish baked apples with almond filling

Mandelfyllda stekta äpplen

6 servings

  1 cup ground almonds
  ¼ cup sugar
  ¼ cup water
  2 egg whites
  6 baking apples
  2 tablespoons margarine or
      butter, melted
  ½ cup dried bread crumbs

In an electric blender, combine almonds, sugar, water, unbeaten egg whites; blend to a smooth paste. Set aside. Peel apples and core almost to the bottom. Brush apples with melted margarine and roll in bread crumbs. Fill cored apples with the almond paste. If any margarine, bread crumbs or almond paste remain, spread on top of apples. Place apples, sides just touching, in 8″ or 9″ pie pan. Bake in a moderate oven (350°) 30 to 40 minutes, or until apples test fork-tender. Serve with custard

Note: Marzipan may be used instead of almond paste.

Apples grow the world over, but each country makes its own special filling for baked apples. Delicate, bittersweet almond-flavored filling blends deliciously with sweet Scandinavian apples.

Swedish custard

Vaniljsås

4 to 6 servings

  3 egg yolks
  ¼ cup sugar
  1½ cups heavy cream
  1 teaspoon vanilla extract

In top of double boiler over boiling water, beat egg yolks, sugar, 1 cup heavy cream and vanilla. Cook until thick, beating constantly. Remove from heat; stir vigorously until the custard is cool. Whip remaining half cup of cream; fold into custard. Chill.

Norwegian fruit jelly with cream

Rödgröd med flöde

4 servings

1 pint red currants
1 pint raspberries
2 cups water
½ cup sugar
1 tablespoon cornstarch
2 tablespoons water
1 teaspoon vanilla extract

In a large saucepan, rinse fruit. Combine fruit and water; simmer over medium heat about 10 minutes. Drain; stir in sugar. Blend cornstarch and water into a smooth paste. Add cornstarch to fruit, stirring constantly. Bring mixture to a boil; cook 3 minutes. Remove from heat and stir in vanilla. Sieve mixture, if desired. Chill. Serve with cream and decorate with blanched almonds, if desired.

Swedish whipped farina

Klappgröt

6 servings

2½ cups water
1 (6 ounce) can frozen concentrate for punch
4 tablespoons farina

In a saucepan, combine water and punch concentrate; bring to a boil. Sprinkle farina into boiling mixture; stir vigorously. Simmer over low heat until farina is cooked, about 5 minutes. Pour mixture into 1½-quart bowl. Beat with an egg beater or hand electric mixer for about 1 minute at a time, at intervals of about 5 minutes, until pudding is fluffy and cool. Chill. Serve with milk or cream if desired.

Swedish rhubarb cream

Rabarberkräm

4 to 6 servings

4 cups rhubarb, peeled and cut into 1½" pieces
2 cups water
¼ cup sugar
3 tablespoons cornstarch
3 tablespoons water

In a large saucepan, combine rhubarb and water; cook over medium heat until tender. Stir in ¼ cup sugar and taste; add more sugar if desired. Blend cornstarch and water into a smooth paste. Add cornstarch to fruit, stirring constantly. Bring mixture to a boil; cook 3 minutes; cool. Chill well before serving.

Swedish berry cream

Bärkräm

6 to 8 servings

1 pint fresh strawberries, raspberries, blueberries or gooseberries (mixture)
2½ cups water
2 tablespoons sugar
3 tablespoons cornstarch
3 tablespoons water

Rinse berries. In a large saucepan, combine berries and water; simmer over medium he 2 to 3 minutes. Stir in sugar. Blend cornstarch and water into a smooth paste. Add cornstarch to berries, stirring constantly. Bring mixture to a boil; cook 3 minutes. Chill.

'Light and airy like a summer's cloud' – Swedish whipped farina is a popular dessert, especially with youngsters.

Danish applesauce

Aeblegröd

6 to 8 servings

   2 *pounds apples, peeled, cored*
     and cubed
¼ *cup water*
  2 *tablespoons white wine*
  1 *tablespoon sugar*

In a large saucepan, cook apples
with water until just tender; stir
in wine. Mash, do not sieve.
Add sugar and taste; add more
sugar if desired. Chill.

Norwegian rice porridge

Risgrynsgröt

4 to 6 servings

   3 *cups cooked rice*
4½ *cups milk*
   1 *tablespoon margarine or*
     butter
⅛ *teaspoon salt*
  2–3 *tablespoons sugar*

In a large heavy saucepan,
combine well drained rice with
milk. Cook, covered, over low
heat until milk is absorbed;
stir occasionally. Stir in
margarine, salt and sugar. Chill.
Serve with cream or apple
compote.

Danish lemon delight

Kan ikke lade vaere

12 servings

 10 *eggs, separated*
  1 *cup sugar*
  1 *envelope unflavored gelatin*
½ *cup water*
½ *cup lemon juice*

Beat egg yolks and sugar
together with electric mixer
until well blended. Sprinkle
gelatin over water in small
saucepan. Place saucepan over
low heat. Cook until gelatin is
melted about 2 to 3 minutes.
Let cool slightly, then beat
gradually into egg yolk mixture.
Beat in the lemon juice. In a
large bowl, beat egg whites until
stiff; fold into yolk mixture.
Pour into a glass bowl. Chill
until set.

Norwegian caramelcream

Karamellpudding

6 to 8 servings

  2 *cups sugar*
  3 *tablespoons boiling water*
  3 *egg yolks*
  2 *tablespoons sugar*
  1 *cup milk*
  1 *teaspoon vanilla extract*
½ *cup heavy cream*
  3 *cups puréed applesauce*

In cast-iron skillet or heavy
saucepan, melt sugar over very
low heat; stir until completely
melted and golden brown.
Remove from heat. Carefully
add boiling water to melted
sugar; stir mixture until well
blended. Combine egg yolks and
2 tablespoons of sugar, milk and
vanilla in top of double-boiler.
With wire-whip, beat mixture
until foamy; cook until hot.
Beating constantly, (do not use
electric mixer) add melted sugar,
now cooled to "soft-ball" stage
to custard mixture. Continue to
beat until mixture cooks.
Remove from heat and continue
beating until mixture has cooled
completely. Beat cream and fold
into cooled custard mixture.
Chill. Serve cold over
applesauce.

Norwegian rice porridge

Swedish egg waffles

Äggvåfflor

4 servings

- 1 cup all purpose flour
- 1 teaspoon baking powder
- 2 eggs, separated
- 1¼ cups heavy cream
- ¼ cup melted margarine or butter

In a large bowl, combine flour and baking powder. In a small bowl, beat egg yolks with cream; add to flour. Blend until smooth. Stir in margarine. Beat egg whites until stiff but not dry; carefully fold into batter. Heat waffle iron; brush lightly with a little melted margarine. Pour batter into center of lower half until it spreads about 1″ from edges. Bring cover down gently. Bake at medium heat until waffle iron stops steaming. Serve immediately with sugar, jam or whipped cream if desired.

Swedish cream waffles

Frasvåfflor

4 servings

- 1¼ cups flour
- 1 cup cold water
- ¼ teaspoon salt
- ¼ cup melted margarine or butter
- 1¾ cups heavy cream

In a bowl, mix flour, water, salt and margarine into a smooth batter. Whip cream until stiff; fold into batter. Chill batter about 1 hour. Heat waffle iron; brush lightly with a little melted margarine. Pour batter into center of lower half until it spreads about 1″ from edges. Bring cover down gently. Bake at medium heat until waffle iron stops steaming. Serve immediately with sugar, jam or fruit.

Swedish baked pancake

Ugnspannkaka

8 to 10 servings

- 2 eggs
- 2½ cups milk
- ½ teaspoon salt
- 2 teaspoons sugar
- 1½ cups sifted flour

In a medium bowl, beat eggs with 1 cup of the milk until well blended. Stir in salt, sugar and flour to make a smooth batter. Stir in remainder of milk; blend until smooth. Set batter aside for 10 minutes. Butter a 12″ × 8″ × 2″ baking dish. Stir batter and pour into prepared pan. Bake in a hot oven (400°) for 30 minutes or until pancake is golden brown and puffy. Serve immediately with jam or fruit purée.

Finnish rice fritters

Klatkage

4 servings

- 1 cup cooked rice, cold
- 2 eggs
- 2 tablespoons raisins
- ¼ teaspoon grated lemon rind
- 2 tablespoons chopped almon
- 2–3 tablespoons flour
- 4 tablespoons margarine or butter
  Powdered sugar
  Jam or jelly

Combine rice, eggs, raisins, lemon rind, almonds and flour. Form mixture into small cakes. Melt margarine in skillet; fry cakes in margarine on both sides. Sprinkle with powdered sugar and serve with jam or jell

The pancake is a Swedish specialty, the perfect dessert on a chilling winter's day.

Norwegian poor knights

Arme riddere

4 servings

     2 eggs
 ½ cup milk
     8 slices white bread, without crusts
 ¼ cup dried bread crumbs
     2 tablespoons sugar
     2 teaspoons cinnamon
     2 tablespoons margarine or butter
        Jam, jelly or powdered sugar

Beat eggs and milk; dip bread slices in mixture. Combine bread crumbs, sugar, and cinnamon. Sprinkle on each side of bread slices. Heat margarine on griddle; sauté bread slices on both sides until golden brown. Spread with jam or jelly or sprinkle with powdered sugar before serving.

Swedish crisp pancakes

Fraspannkakor

4 servings

      2 eggs, separated
 1¼ cups water
  ¼ teaspoon salt
      1 tablespoon sugar
      1 cup sifted all-purpose flour
  ½ cup heavy cream, whipped
      1 tablespoon margarine or butter

In a medium bowl, beat egg yolks, water, salt, sugar and flour until well blended. Fold in whipped cream. Beat egg whites until stiff; fold into batter. Rub a crêpe pan or small skillet lightly with margarine. Add 3 to 4 tablespoons batter; tip pan and let batter spread over the bottom. Cook over medium heat just until bubbles appear on surface. Turn; cook until browned. Serve with puréed fruit if desired.

Swedish caramel mold

Brylépudding

6 servings

     1 cup sugar
     6 eggs
     2 cups light cream
 ½ teaspoon vanilla
 ½ cup cream, whipped
     2 tablespoons brandy

In a heavy pan, melt ½ cup of the sugar over very low heat until just golden brown. Pour into bottom of a 9″ ring mold; spread to cover entire bottom. Beat eggs well; add ½ cup sugar, cream and vanilla. Pour into mold. Set mold in a pan of hot (not boiling) water; bake in a moderate oven (325°) 1 hour or until knife inserted in center comes out clean. Cool. Dip mold quickly into a pan of hot water and unmold. Whip cream and brandy together until soft peaks form. Serve over molded dessert.

Danish veiled country lass

Bondepige med slör

8 servings

 ¼ cup margarine or butter
     4 cups pumpernickel bread, finely crumbled
     2 tablespoons sugar
     3 cups applesauce
     1 cup heavy cream, whipped
 ½ cup raspberry jam or jelly

Melt margarine in large skillet; stir in bread crumbs, fry until crisp. Stir in sugar until well blended; set aside. In bottom of pretty glass bowl, layer ⅓ of bread mixture. Cover with 1½ cups applesauce. Top applesauce with second ⅓ of bread mixture; top with remaining 1½ cups applesauce. Top second layer of applesauce with remaining bread mixture. Top with layer of whipped cream. Make 8 pools in whipped cream; fill each pool with raspberry jam or jelly. Chill.

Swedish crisp pancakes

Cakes & Pastries

Finnish shortbread

Finska pinnar

4 dozen cookies

2½ cups flour
½ cup sugar
¼ cup finely chopped almonds
¾ cup margarine or butter, softened
1 egg, slightly beaten
2 tablespoons sugar
Coarsely chopped almonds

Combine flour, sugar, almonds and margarine; knead into a firm dough. (If necessary, add a few drops of water to make dough easy to handle.) Use about 1 teaspoonful of dough for each cookie. Roll dough into a log about 2″ long. Dip in egg, then in sugar and chopped almonds. Bake on buttered cookie sheet in a hot oven (400°) about 10 minutes.

Bread and almond filled buns

Semlor

10 buns

1 recipe plain buns, **this page**
¼ cup cream or milk
¾ cup ground almonds
⅔ cup sugar
Confectioner's sugar

Prepare recipe for buns; cool. Cut a lid from each bun and remove inside crumbs. Soak crumbs in cream or milk. Mix almonds and sugar with soaked crumbs. Fill buns; replace lids. Heat in moderate oven (350°) for a few minutes. Sprinkle with confectioner's sugar.

Almond filled buns

Fyllda bullar

10 buns

1 recipe plain buns, **this page**
½ cup almond paste (marzipan)
1 cup heavy cream, whipped
Confectioner's sugar

Prepare recipe for buns; cool. Blend almond paste and whipped cream. Let stand in refrigerator at least one hour. Stir. Cut a lid from each bun, and make a small cavity; fill with almond mixture. Replace lids and sprinkle with confectioner's sugar. Serve immediately. (If not used immediately, filled buns should be refrigerated.)

Swedish plain buns

Släta bullar

10 buns

2 packages dry yeast
1 cup light cream
1 cup margarine or butter
¼ cup sugar
¼ cup ground almonds
1 teaspoon ground cardamom
3¼ cups flour
1 egg
Beaten egg

Blend yeast and ½ cup of the cream. Melt margarine. Add remaining ½ cup cream and hea[t] mixture until lukewarm; add to yeast. Stir in sugar, ground almonds, cardamom, half of the flour, and egg. Add remaining flour gradually, stirring constantly. Knead dough until smooth. Sprinkle a little flour o[n] top, cover with a cloth and allow dough to rise until double in size. Turn dough onto a lightly-floured surface; knead until smooth again. Divide dough into 10 equal pieces and shape into round, smooth buns without cracks. Place buns on greased baking sheet; let rise until doubled. Brush carefully with beaten egg. Bake in hot oven (400°) for 10 minutes.

Swedish plain buns

Danish marzipan cakes

Kransekager

25 cakes

1⅔ cups ground almonds
1¼ cups sugar
3 egg-whites, lightly beaten
  Confectioner's sugar

In a saucepan, combine almonds, sugar and egg-whites. Beating vigorously, simmer the mixture slowly over low heat until it thickens and retains its shape. Remove from heat and cool. Divide dough into 25 equal pieces; shape into small loaves about 2½" long. Roll loaves in confectioner's sugar. Press gently to make the tops pointed. Bake on a buttered cookie sheet, lightly sprinkled with flour, in a hot oven (400°) about 6 minutes. The cakes should set on the surface and brown lightly but remain soft inside.

Swedish crown cake

Kronans kaka

4 servings

2 eggs
½ cup granulated sugar
¼ cup margarine or butter
⅔ cup ground almonds
2 boiled, cold medium
  potatoes, grated
2 tablespoons bread crumbs

In a bowl, beat the eggs and sugar until thick and foamy. In another bowl, cream margarine, add ground almonds, then gradually add egg mixture. Blend well; add potatoes. Grease an 8-inch cake pan and sprinkle with bread crumbs shaking off excess crumbs. Pour batter into pan. Bake in a moderate oven (350°) 25 minutes. Cool. Serve cake with lemon sauce, if desired.

Danish apple cake

Aeblekage

4 to 6 servings

2 tablespoons sugar
½ teaspoon vanilla
1 (16 ounce) can applesauce
1¼ cups dried bread crumbs
½ cup melted margarine or
  butter
1 cup cream, whipped
  Jelly

Add sugar and vanilla to applesauce. Butter an ovenproof dish; alternate layers of bread crumbs, and applesauce ending with bread crumbs. Pour melted margarine over all. Bake in a very hot oven (450°) about 25 to 30 minutes. Serve hot topped with whipped cream and jelly.

Swedish cheese cake

Småländsk ostkaka

8 servings

2 cups cottage cheese
¼ cup flour
3 eggs
¼ cup sugar
2 cups light cream
½ cup coarsely chopped
  almonds, lightly toasted

Stir cottage cheese by hand or with mixer, until granular. Add flour, eggs, sugar, cream, and almonds; mix well. Grease a 10" fluted pie pan or 8" square baking pan. Pour in mixture; bake in a moderate oven (350°) 50 to 60 minutes, or until knife inserted in center comes out clean.
Garnish with whipped cream and jelly.

Smaland is a land of rich green pastures, producing sweet cream in abundance. Small wonder, then, that the Smaland farmer's wife makes Scandinavia's smoothest and sweetest cottage cheese and cream cakes.

Swedish cheese cake

Norwegian chiffon cake

Englekake

8″ or 9″ tube cake

  1 *cup cake flour*
1½ *teaspoons baking powder*
  ¾ *cup sugar*
  ½ *teaspoon salt*
  ¼ *cup vegetable oil*
  2 *egg yolks*
  4 *tablespoons orange juice*
  1 *teaspoon grated orange rind*
  4 *egg whites*
  ¼ *teaspoon cream of tartar*

In a large mixing bowl, sift flour, baking powder, sugar and salt. Make a well in center; pour in oil, egg yolks, orange juice and rind. Beat with electric mixer 2 minutes until satiny smooth. Beat egg whites and cream of tartar until stiff. Add batter to egg whites a little at a time, gently folding in with rubber spatula until evenly blended. *Do not beat.* Pour in ungreased 8″ or 9″ tube pan. Bake in a slow oven (325°) 35 minutes; then increase heat to 350° and bake until top springs back when pressed lightly with finger (about 5 minutes). Invert until cold. Loosen from sides with knife and remove carefully.

Finnish caramel-iced cake

Kinuskikakku

10 servings

  1 *recipe caramel icing*
  ¾ *cup margarine or butter*
  1 *chiffon cake,*
  3 *tablespoons lemon juice*
  3 *tablespoons water*
  2 *tablespoons chopped pistachio nuts*

Prepare caramel icing according to directions; cool. Cream margarine until fluffy; blend into icing. Slice the cake horizontally into 3 equal layers. Combine lemon juice and water; sprinkle over each layer. Spread top of each layer with icing, and stack. Ice top layer and sides. Sprinkle with pistachio nuts.

Caramel icing:
  ¾ *cup sugar*
1½ *cups cream*
  5 *teaspoons cocoa*
  5 *teaspoons dark molasses*

In saucepan, combine all ingredients. Cook over low heat until mixture forms a soft ball in cold water. Cool slightly before using.

Marstrand cookies

Marstrandskex

6 dozen cookies

  1 *cup potato flour*
1¾ *cups flour*
  2 *teaspoons baking powder*
  1 *cup granulated sugar*
  1 *cup heavy cream*
  1 *cup melted margarine or butter*

In a bowl, sift together the flours, and baking powder. Add sugar, cream and margarine; knead quickly. Chill dough until firm. Roll dough thinly, about ⅛″ thick; prick in several places with a fork. With a pastry cutter, cut out cookies of about 2½″ in diameter. Bake cookies on buttered cookie sheet in a moderate oven (350°) about 10 minutes, or until very lightly browned.

Finnish caramel-iced cake

Finnish light sponge cake

Sokerikakku

1 layer or 1 small tube cake

- 1   cup cake flour
- 1¼   teaspoons baking powder
      Pinch of salt
- 2   eggs, separated
- ¾   cup sugar
- ¼   cup hot water
- ½   teaspoon vanilla

Sift together flour, baking powder and salt. Beat egg whites until they stand in soft peaks. Gradually beat in ¼ cup of the sugar. Add hot water and vanilla to egg yolks; beat until thick. Beat in remaining ½ cup sugar. Pour egg yolks over whites, cutting and folding until well blended. Fold in flour mixture. Spoon batter into unbuttered 9″ layer or 7- or 8″ tube pan. Bake in a moderate oven (350°) 20 to 30 minutes, or until cake springs back when pressed lightly with finger. Invert on wire cake rack; let stand until cold. Loosen edges with sharp knife; ease out of pan.

Swedish cream cake

Gräddtårta

8 servings

- 3   9″ sponge cake layers
- 1   cup applesauce or jam
- 1½   cups prepared packaged vanilla pudding
- 2   cups heavy cream
- ½   teaspoon vanilla
- 2   tablespoons sugar
- 20   strawberries

Spread one cake layer with ½ of the applesauce or jam, then ½ of the pudding. Place second layer on top; spread with remaining applesauce and pudding. Top with third layer. Whip cream; add vanilla and sugar. Spread cream over cake; garnish with strawberries.

Swedish brown spice cookies

Bruna bröd

5 dozen cookies

- 1¾   cups flour
- 1   teaspoon baking powder
- ½   cup brown sugar
- ½   cup finely chopped almonds
- 1   teaspoon cinnamon
- 1   teaspoon ground cardamom
- 1   cup, plus 2 tablespoons soft margarine or butter
- 1   egg yolk
      Granulated sugar

In a large bowl mix all ingredients except granulated sugar. Knead quickly; chill. Shape dough into a long roll ½″ wide. Cut off small pieces of dough and roll into balls; dip into granulated sugar. Bake cookies on a buttered cookie sheet in a moderately hot oven (375°) about 12 minutes.

It may be because of the long, dark winter that keeps people indoors, but Scandinavian baking, which requires hours of devotion, has achieved a level unsurpassed anywhere in the world. The most delicious things emerge from the oven. Wheat and rye bread come in the most fantastic forms: round, flat, oval, braided and ring-shaped. The variations in sweet cakes are even more incredible, not only for festive holidays, but for breakfast and coffee time, in fact sweet cakes for every minute of the day. Swedish cakes in particular are often heavily flavored with such Eastern spices as ginger and cardamon. The tradition was probably inherited from the adventurous Vikings, who voyaged along the great rivers of Russia to reach Constantinople, and returned heavily laden with priceless Eastern spices.

Swedish cream cake

74

Danish pastries

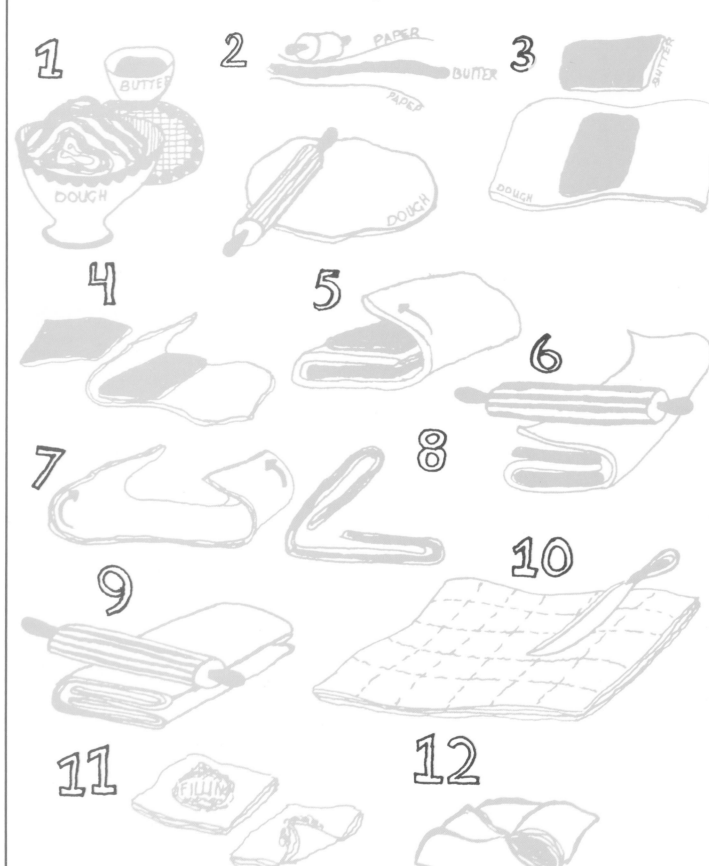

Danish pastries

Wienerbrød

40 pastries

1¼ cups cold butter
½ cup flour
2 envelopes dry yeast
½ cup warm water
½ cup cold milk
¼ cup sugar
1 egg, beaten
3¼ cups flour

Filling:
1 cup almonds or hazelnuts
1¼ cups confectioner's sugar
2 egg whites or
1 lightly-beaten egg

Chop together cold butter and ½ cup flour; knead until mixture sticks together. Refrigerate to harden. Dissolve yeast in warm water; add cold milk. Stir in sugar, egg, and half the flour. Gradually add remaining flour, stirring constantly. Knead dough until smooth and shiny; set aside. Roll butter mixture between wax paper into an oblong about 7″ × 14″. Place on cookie sheet; refrigerate. Roll out dough on lightly floured board into a square about 14″ × 14″. Place butter oblong over half of the dough, remove wax paper, and fold other half over it. Press lightly with rolling pin; roll doubled dough in the other direction into oblong strip. Fold dough into 3 sections— fold one edge in ⅓ of the way, then the other. Roll again into an oblong. Repeat the rolling and folding twice more. (In all, dough should be rolled and folded 3 times.) Flour board between rolling, and brush off any surplus flour from dough. If dough shows a tendency to become sticky, discontinue the rolling and refrigerate 10 to 15 minutes or until dough becomes firm. After third rolling and folding, cover dough with a clean towel; refrigerate for 15 minutes. Grind nuts. Add the confectioner's sugar; stir in enough egg white or beaten egg to make mixture smooth and stiff. Make pastries into desired shapes, crescents, bow knots, braids, etc., using about 1 teaspoon nut filling on each. Place pastries on buttered baking sheets and let stand about 15 minutes in a cool place. Bake in a hot oven (400°) about 15 minutes. Cool. If desired, drizzle with confectioner's glaze.

Note: Marzipan may be used instead of almond filling.

The finest Danish cake is 'Wienerbrød', or 'Viennese rolls' (but what we know as Danish pastries), made from paperthin, crispy, light layers of dough. Danish bakers apparently learned to prepare this buttery yeast dough from the Viennese. But in Vienna itself people call Wienerbrød 'Copenhagen pastries', and it is the unique quality of famous Danish butter that gives this cake its incredible lightness.

Danish pastries in an early stage of their preparation, and ready for serving

Swedish Lucia gingersnaps

Lucia-pepparkakor

3 dozen

  1 *(14½-ounce) package gingerbread mix*
  ⅓ *cup lukewarm water*
  ⅛ *teaspoon lemon extract*

Blend ingredients. Chill dough.
Roll dough out on floured
board. Cut into desired shape.
Place on buttered cookie sheet
and bake in moderately hot
oven (375°) 8 to 10 minutes.

Swedish country lasses

Bondkakor

5 dozen cookies

  2 *cups flour*
1½ *teaspoons baking powder*
  ¾ *cup sugar*
  ¾ *cup coarsely chopped almonds*
  1 *tablespoon molasses*
  ⅔ *cup margarine or butter*

In a large mixing bowl, blend
all ingredients; knead to make a
smooth, firm dough. Divide
dough into 3 parts; roll into
cylinders, about 1½″ in
diameter. Refrigerate until firm
Cut cylinders into ¼″ slices.
Bake on a greased cookie sheet
in a hot oven (400°) about
10 minutes.

*Lucia gingersnaps (above right)
and country lasses (above left)*

Swedish glogg

Glögg

8 servings

1 (26-ounce) bottle dry red
  wine or
1 (26-ounce) bottle aquavit
1 cup sugar
1 stick cinnamon
5 cloves
6 cardamom seeds, crushed
1 orange peel spiral
½ cup slivered almonds
½ cup raisins

Combine wine, sugar, cinnamon,
cloves, cardamom and orange
peel in saucepan; stir to blend.
Let stand 3 to 4 hours. Heat, but
do not boil. Light with a match
and pour burning into heatproof
cups containing a few almonds
and raisins.

Swedish mumma

Mumma

4 to 5 servings

1 (12-ounce) bottle dark
  beer, chilled
1 (12-ounce) bottle light
  beer, chilled
1 (12-ounce) bottle ale, chilled
¼ cup gin

Combine all ingredients in a
large well chilled pitcher; stir to
blend. Serve immediately.

Fruit juice glogg

Saftglögg

6 servings

2 cups apple juice
1 cup grape juice
2 tablespoons sugar
1 stick cinnamon
4 cloves
1 orange peel spiral
⅓ cup raisins
⅓ cup slivered almonds

In saucepan, combine juices,
sugar, spices and orange peel
spiral; bring just to a boil.
Place several raisins and almonds
in punch cups. Remove cloves,
cinnamon and orange peel
spiral from juice; pour into cups.

Danish wine cooler

Vinbowle

12 servings

2 orange slices
1 lemon, sliced
¼ cup sugar
¼ cup brandy
  Ice
1 (26-ounce) bottle dry white
  wine, chilled
1 (12-ounce) bottle club
  soda, chilled

Place fruit in tall pitcher;
sprinkle with sugar. Press fruit
with back of spoon to release
flavor. Add brandy. Chill 1 to 2
hours. Add ice and wine; stir to
blend. Add club soda just before
serving.

Norwegian eggcream

Eggedosis

Makes 1 quart

10 egg yolks
½ cup sugar
1 cup brandy
  Nutmeg

Beat egg yolks and sugar
together until thick and
creamy, about 5 to 7 minutes.
Gradually add brandy; beat
until well blended. Pour into
punch bowl or individual
punch cups. Sprinkle with
nutmeg.

Traditional Christmas dishes

The delicacies crammed into the
store room of a Scandinavian
farmhouse – freshly brewed beer,
chimney-smoked sausages and
hams, sweet butter and marinated
fish. All of them are on display
in abundance during the festive
Christmas season.

In Norway, Sweden, Denmark, or Finland, Christmas is a feast of light and warmth in the house, of crackling logs in the fireplace, of flickering candles in the Christmas tree and wreaths, of warmth and pleasure and of groaning tables that all but collapse under the weight of the food heaped on them. Baking begins weeks in advance, and different kinds of breads, often in the ancient, traditional forms of wreaths and sun rays are a particular speciality. In remote farms people brew Christmas beer and distill akvavit. Lutfish go into their wooden tubs and pigs and geese are killed. And when the great season arrives on Christmas Eve, the table is finally laid for twelve days of feasting. Traditional Christmas dishes are lutfish and rice porridge, ham, braised goose filled with apples and served with red cabbage, liver paté, spicy sausages, head cheese and cookies and cakes without end. The Norwegians are fond of spareribs served with sauerkraut; the Danes always expect goose; the Swedes and the Finns prefer ham, braised and prepared in a pastry shell. For drink there is foamy beer or Glögg, a steamy, hot concoction made with wine, brandy or akvavit, and fragrant spices. In Norway it is served with thin pancakes made from rye flour and wrapped around slices of goat cheese.

Swedish liver paté

Leverpastej

2 loaves

1 pound pork liver
1 quart water
1 tablespoon salt
1 pound bacon
4 anchovy fillets
1 teaspoon margarine or butter
1 tablespoon finely chopped onion
½ teaspoon salt
1 teaspoon white pepper
3 eggs
1 tablespoon cornstarch
2 tablespoons cold water
2 cups heavy cream
¼ pound bacon slices, if desired

In 2-quart bowl, soak liver in water and salt about 2 to 3 hours; drain. Put liver through fine blade of meat grinder, alternating with 1 pound bacon strips and anchovies. In small skillet melt margarine; sauté onion in margarine until transparent. Add salt, pepper, eggs, cornstarch mixed with water, and cream. Beat with fork until smooth. Line two 9″ × 5″ × 3″ loaf pans with greased aluminum foil or slices of bacon. Put 3½ cups mixture into each pan; cover with aluminum foil. Place pans in large baking pan; fill to a depth of 1″ with hot water. Bake in a moderate oven (350°) about 1 hour or until knife inserted near center shows no pink meat or juices. Chill well. Unmold. Serve in slices on bread or lettuce leaves.

Liver paté in aspic

Leverpastej i gelé

2 loaves

1 recipe liver paté
4 beef bouillon cubes
3 cups boiling water
4 envelopes unflavored gelatin
1 cup cold water
2 hard-cooked eggs, sliced

Prepare liver paté, chill well; unmold. Remove bacon slices, if used. Dissolve bouillon cubes in boiling water. Soften gelatin in cold water; dissolve in hot bouillon. Pour about ⅛″ gelatin mixture into each 9″ × 5″ × 3″ loaf pan. Arrange egg slices in an attractive pattern in gelatin. Allow to chill in refrigerator or over ice cubes until set. Place liver paté on layer of eggs and gelatin. Pour remaining gelatin mixture over and around paté. Cover and chill until firm, at least 4 hours. Loosen carefully, dip into hot water, unmold onto serving platter.

Danish herring salad

Sildesalat

6 servings

1 (1 pound) jar pickled schmaltz herring, meat removed from bones, cut into ½″ cubes
4 medium, diced, cooked potatoes
1 cup diced pickled beets
1 cup diced dill pickle
2 medium tart apples, peeled and diced
1 tablespoon finely chopped onion
Dash white pepper
½ cup sour cream
½ teaspoon salt
Lettuce leaves

Combine all ingredients. Taste and add salt, if needed; chill. Serve cold on lettuce leaves, garnished, if desired, with parsley and sliced hard-cooked egg.

Swedish jellied veal

Kalvsylta

10 to 12 servings

1 *(4 to 4½ pound) shoulder,
  neck, breast, rump or leg
  of veal with bone*
9 *cups water*
1 *tablespoon salt*
10 *peppercorns*
5 *allspice berries*
1 *bay leaf*
2 *cloves*
1 *medium onion, peeled and
  quartered*
2 *tablespoons vinegar*
4 *envelopes unflavored gelatin*
1 *cup cold water*

Place meat in 6 to 8 quart
saucepan. Cover with water;
add salt, peppercorns, allspice,
bay leaf, cloves and onion.
Cover, bring to a boil; reduce
heat; simmer 1½ hours or until
meat is loosened from bones.
Remove meat; allow to cool.
Remove bones and gristle,
return to bouillon and simmer
gently another hour. Dice meat
and set aside (about 2½ cups).
Strain bouillon; measure and if
necessary, add water to make
7 cups. Return to saucepan.
Correct seasonings. Stir in
vinegar. Bring just to a boil;
reduce heat; simmer. Soften
gelatin in cold water; dissolve in
the hot broth. Chill in
refrigerator or over ice cubes,
stirring frequently, until
consistency of thick egg white.
Stir in reserved diced meat. Pour
into 2 loaf pans or 1½ quart
molds which have been rinsed
with cold water. Chill until
firm. Unmold.

Swedish delicatessen meatballs

Delikatessköttbullar

50 to 75 meatballs

½ *pound ground beef*
½ *pound ground veal*
¼ *pound ground pork or
  sausage*
1 *teaspoon salt*
¼ *teaspoon white pepper*
1 *egg yolk*
½ *cup fine dry bread crumbs*
1 *cup half-and-half*
1 *tablespoon chopped onion*
¼ *cup margarine or butter
  Flour*

Combine meats, salt, pepper,
egg yolk, crumbs and cream;
mix well with fork. Cook onion
in 1 tablespoon of the margarine
until transparent; mix into meat
mixture. Form small meat balls
with two teaspoons; roll in flour.
In large frying pan over
moderately high heat, brown
meat balls on all sides in
remaining margarine. Drain on
paper towels.

Swedish roast goose

Stekt gås

8 servings

1 *(12 pound) goose*
½ *lemon*
1 *teaspoon salt*
¼ *teaspoon black pepper*
8 *apples, cored and quartered*
30 *pitted prunes*
2 *teaspoons caraway seed*
2 *tablespoons cornstarch*
2 *cups chicken bouillon*

Wash and dry goose. Remove
any excess fat inside cavity.
Rub neck and body cavities of
goose lightly with lemon, salt,
and pepper. Fill cavities with
apples, prunes and caraway seed.
Skewer openings shut. Place on
rack in shallow roasting pan,
breast side down. Roast in a
slow oven (325°) about 4 to 4½
hours, or until tender when
pierced with a fork and juices
are light yellow, not pink. Drain
fat during roasting. Remove
goose; keep warm. Skim off fat
from pan drippings. Mix
cornstarch and bouillon; add to
pan. Cook over medium heat,
stirring and scraping browned
bits, until thickened. Discard
stuffing. Serve gravy with goose.

*An assortment of delicious
breads, sweet butter and cheese
is a particular specialty of the
Christmas season throughout
Scandinavia.*

Finnish turnip pie

Lanttulaatikko

6 servings

- 2 pounds yellow turnip, peeled and cut into ½" cubes
- ½ teaspoon salt
- 1½ cups fine dry bread crumbs
- 1 cup half-and-half
- 1 tablespoon sugar
  Dash ground white pepper
- ⅛ teaspoon ground nutmeg
- 2 eggs, lightly beaten
- 2 tablespoons margarine or butter

Cook turnip in just enough salted water to cover until tender, about 30 minutes. Drain and mash. Stir in 1 cup of the bread crumbs, half-and-half, sugar, pepper and nutmeg. Taste and add salt, if needed. Stir in beaten eggs. Use part of the margarine to grease a 9" round cake tin, about 2" deep. Coat with 1 to 2 tablespoons of remaining crumbs. Spread turnip mixture in pan, sprinkle with remaining crumbs and dot with remaining margarine. Bake in a slow oven (325°) 1 hour or until lightly browned.

Finnish sweetened potato pudding

Imellytetty perunalaatikko

4 servings

- 6 medium boiled potatoes, hot
- 4 tablespoons flour
- 2 tablespoons sugar
- 1 tablespoon salt
- 3 cups milk
- 4 tablespoons margarine or butter

Slice potatoes into buttered 2-quart mold. Sprinkle mixture of flour and sugar over each layer. Add salt, milk and margarine. Bake in a moderate oven (350°) for 40 minutes or until golden brown.

Norwegian red cabbage

Rödkål

6 servings

- 2 tablespoons margarine or butter
- 2 pounds red cabbage, finely shredded
- 2 medium apples, peeled and sliced
- 1 medium onion, chopped
- 2 teaspoons caraway seed, crushed
- 1 teaspoon salt
- 2 tablespoons maple or dark corn syrup
- ¼ cup vinegar
- 2 tablespoons water

In a large heavy saucepan, melt margarine. Add cabbage, apples, onion, caraway seed, salt, syrup, vinegar and water. Cover; bring to a boil, tossing lightly occasionally to blend. Reduce heat and simmer about 45 minutes or until tender. Stir occasionally; add a little water, if needed. Remove cover during last 10 minutes to allow any excess liquid to evaporate. Serve with Christmas ham, roast goose or duck.

Norwegian braised red cabbage

Brunkål

4 to 6 servings

- 4 tablespoons margarine or butter
- 2 pounds red cabbage, finely shredded
- 2 tablespoons sugar
- 1 tablespoon lemon juice
- ¾ cup cranberry juice cocktail
- 1 tart apple, peeled, cored and grated

Melt margarine in a non-metallic saucepan. Add cabbage; sauté 2 to 3 minutes, tossing lightly. Add sugar, lemon juice, cranberry juice and apple. Cover and simmer for about 1 hour or until tender, stirring occasionally.

Swedish Christmas ham

Griljerad skinka

6 servings

  1 (3-pound) canned ham
  1 egg, lightly beaten
  2 tablespoons prepared
     mustard
  1 tablespoon sugar
  2 tablespoons fine, dry bread
     crumbs
  4 tablespoons water
  2 tablespoons tart jelly
     (crabapple, red currant, or
     seedless raspberry)

Place ham in baking pan. Bake
in a moderate oven (325°) for
1 hour. Remove from oven;
increase temperature setting to
400°. Mix together the egg,
mustard and sugar; spread over
ham; sprinkle with bread
crumbs. Return to oven about
10 minutes or until crumbs are
golden brown. Place on warm
platter; let rest about 10
minutes before carving.
Meanwhile, add water to
contents of baking pan; stir and
scrape until all brown bits are
loosened. Bring to a boil. Strain
into a small saucepan. Add jelly,
heat until jelly melts. Serve hot
or cold with hot or cold sliced
ham.

Swedish boiled pig's feet

Kokta grisfötter

4 servings

  2 fresh pig's feet (about 1¼
     pounds) washed and cut
     in half lengthwise
     Cold water
  2 tablespoons salt
  1 quart water
  8 white peppercorns
  8 allspice berries

Place pig's feet in large bowl
with water to cover. Cover and
place in refrigerator for 12 hours
or overnight. Rinse. Place in
2-quart saucepan. Cover with
cold water, bring to a boil; pour
off water. Add salt, 1 quart
water and spices to pig's feet in
saucepan. Cover, bring to a boil,
reduce heat; cook about 2½
hours or until bones are
loosened. Pour off liquid. Rinse.
Serve with mustard and pickled
beets.

Finnish ham

Kinkku

12 to 14 servings

  1 (12 to 14 pound) fresh ham
  ½ cup salt
  2 tablespoons sugar
  1 tablespoon saltpetre
 10 quarts water
  8 cups coarse or Kosher salt
  6 cups rye flour
1–1½ cups water
     Bread crumbs

Rub ham all over with mixture
of salt, sugar and saltpetre.
Cover lightly with plastic wrap.
Refrigerate 2 days. Combine
water, coarse salt and
bring to a boil.
Cool. Place ham in extra large
bowl, crock or plastic pail or
basket; pour in cooled salted
water. Make sure ham is
completely covered by water.
Let stand in very cool place 8 to
10 days. Remove ham; rinse in
cold water; pat dry with paper
towel. Mix together flour and
water; roll or pat out into large
square 18″ × 18″. Cover ham
with dough. Place ham on rack
in shallow roasting pan. Bake in
a moderate oven (350°) for
5 hours. Remove crust; sprinkle
ham with bread crumbs. Return
to oven. Bake 10 minutes or
until crumbs are browned and
crisp.

Baked ham with mustard sauce

Glaseret skinke

1 canned ham
   Prepared mustard
   Brown sugar
   Cloves

Place ham in baking pan; do
not remove excess gelatin or
fat. Spread mustard on top
and sides of ham with a knife.
Score ham in diamond pattern
and stud with cloves. Sprinkle
brown sugar in thick layer
over it. Bake at 350°, about 10
minutes per pound. Baste
frequently until brown.

Lutfisk

No one knows how old the Swedish tradition of eating lutfisk at Christmas is. The custom may date back as long ago as the Vikings, and it certainly has its roots in the time before the Reformation when it was traditional to fast before Christmas and eat only fish on Christmas Eve. The preparation of lutfisk (the name means 'lye fish') is very complicated, and the housewife must begin her work in the first week of December. The fish, usually dried cod, is first sawed into pieces and then soaked in a wooden tub in which the water is changed every day. A layer of lime is then sprinkled into the bottom of the tub, the fish is laid on the lime, more lime is sprinkled on top and then covered with a soda solution. A wide plank and a weight are placed on top of the fish, which is left to stand for six days. (In other parts of Scandinavia the process is even more complicated: instead of a soda solution a birchwood broth is used.) Finally the fish must soak for another week in fresh water changed every day. Then the lutfisk can be cooked (always wrapped in a towel) and served as the central dish at the festive Christmas dinner together with potatoes and cream sauce.

Traditionally, red wine is served with lutfisk.

Swedish Christmas punch

Julglögg

12 servings

2 cups aquavit
1 (26-ounce) bottle dry red wine
½ cup sugar
1 cinnamon stick
5 cloves
4 cardamom seeds, crushed
1 orange peel spiral
½ cup slivered almonds
½ cup raisins

Combine aquavit, wine, sugar, spices and orange peel in saucepan. Heat but do not boil. Light with a match and pour burning into glogg glasses or heat-proof cups containing a few almonds and raisins.

Tjinuski caramels

Tjinuskikola

Makes 64–1″ squares

1½ cups sugar
¼ cup cocoa
⅓ cup molasses
1¾ cups milk
¼ cup margarine or butter
1 teaspoon vanilla

In a heavy saucepan, combine sugar, and cocoa. Add molasses, milk and margarine. Cook over moderate heat, stirring constantly, until candy reaches hard ball stage, 248° F. on a candy thermometer. Pour into buttered 8″ square pan. Do not scrape the sides of pan. When partially cooled, mark and cut into 1″ squares. When thoroughly cooled, wrap individually in waxed paper.

Danish rice pudding

Riskrem

6 servings

3 cups milk
½ cup rice or
2 cups pre-cooked rice
½ teaspoon vanilla
¾ cup sugar
2 envelopes gelatine
¼ cup cold water
¼ cup chopped almonds
4 tablespoons margarine or butter
1 cup heavy cream, whipped

Bring milk to a boil. Add rice, vanilla and sugar. Simmer over medium heat until cooked, or if instant rice is used, cover and let stand 5 minutes over lowest heat. Remove from heat and stir in gelatin softened in ¼ cup cold water. Stir in almonds and margarine. Cool. Fold in whipped cream. Pour into a 2-quart mold; chill until set. Unmold and serve cold.

Peter Heering delight

Peter Heering med flødeskum og knuste makroner

8 to 10 servings

1 (6 ounce) package cherry flavoured jelly powder
2 cups boiling water
⅔ cup cold water
1⅓ cup Peter Heering liqueur
1½ cups whipping cream
¼ cup blanched slivered almonds
6 whole almonds

Dissolve jelly powder in 2 cups boiling water. Add cold water and then Peter Heering, mixing thoroughly. Pour mixture into a rinsed ring mold and chill until set. Just before serving, whip the cream and fold in slivered almonds.
Unmold the jelly and fill the centre with the whipped cream. Garnish with whole almonds.

Peter Heering delight

Keeping warm in a cold climate demands plenty of calories. This is one of the reasons why so many sweet things are eaten during the long and bitter northern winter.

Chocolate toffee

Chokladkola

Makes 64–1″ squares

  2 *cups sugar*
  1 *cup dark corn syrup*
  1 *cup evaporated milk*
  3 *(1-ounce) squares*
     unsweetened chocolate, cut
     into small pieces
  1 *tablespoon margarine*
     or butter
  1 *teaspoon vanilla*

In a heavy saucepan, combine
sugar, corn syrup, milk, and
chocolate pieces. Cook over
moderate heat until mixture
reaches the hard ball stage,
248° F. on a candy thermometer.
Stir constantly. Add margarine
and vanilla; stir well. Pour
candy into a buttered 8″ square
pan. Do not scrape the sides of
the pan. When partially cooled,
mark into 1″ squares. When
thoroughly cooled, cut into
squares and wrap individually
in waxed paper.

Finnish chocolate ice

Suklaakakku

48 pieces

  1 *(6-ounce) package*
     semi-sweet chocolate pieces
  3 *tablespoons margarine or*
     butter
  1 *egg*
  1 *tablespoon grated orange*
     peel

Melt chocolate with margarine
in top of double boiler; cool
slightly. Beat egg in a small bowl
with electric mixer. Slowly add
chocolate and orange peel; beat
until thoroughly blended. Drop
from teaspoon onto a buttered
cookie sheet. Chill thoroughly
until firm.

Swedish toffee

Knäck

Makes 64-1″ squares

  1 *cup sugar*
  ¾ *cup heavy cream*
  ¾ *cup molasses*
  ⅓ *cup chopped almonds*
  4 *tablespoons margarine or*
     butter

In a heavy saucepan, combine
sugar, cream, and molasses.
Cook over moderate heat until
candy reaches hard ball stage,
248° F. on the candy
thermometer. Add almonds and
margarine; stir to mix. Pour
into an 8″ square pan. Cool. Cut
into 1″ squares.

Gingerbread house

Alongside the Christmas tree, the pine branches and pine cones, the wreaths and red ribbons which all decorate Swedish homes during the darkest days of the year, the sweet and spicy gingerbread house is always present. It stands there in all its glossy brown sweetness as the symbol of domestic happiness. The gingerbread house is always prepared by the children of the family (but with the expert help of the mother, of course). The mother prepares the dough, which is rolled out to a thin layer. Then the parts of the house are cut out using cardboard forms and the individual pieces are baked in the oven. When the walls and roof forms have been cooled on a rack, they are decorated with colored glaze from a pastry bag: the doors and windows get borders, there are piles of 'snow' for the roof, and decorated paper curtains are hung in the windows. Then the house is put together, with the cardboard forms used as supports. What happier scene can there be than the little gingerbread house, set deep in the snow, a small mirror representing a nearby frozen lake, and pine branches simulating the snow-laden trees surrounding the house.

(See color illustration of Gingerbread house on page 68)

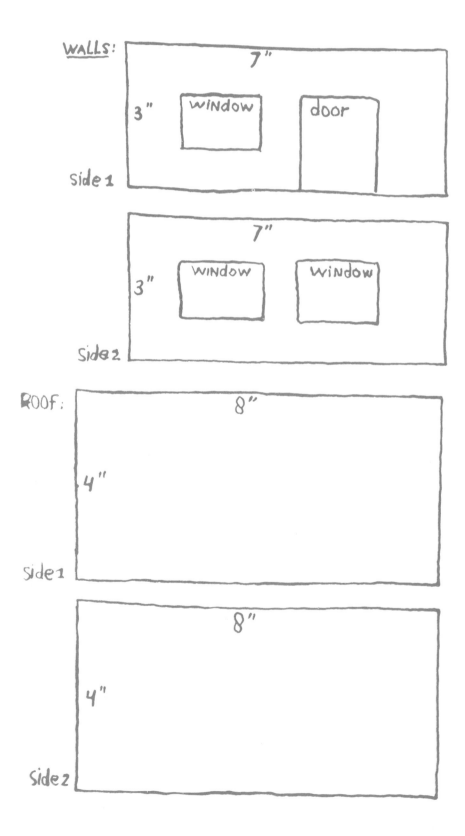

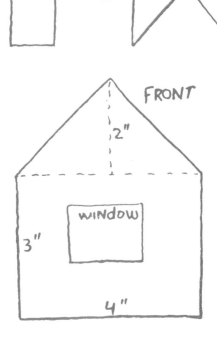

Gingerbread house

Pepparkakshus

1 house

- 1 *cup brown sugar, firmly packed*
- 1 *cup molasses*
- 1 *cup shortening*
- 5 *cups sifted flour*
- 1 *tablespoon baking soda*
- 1 *tablespoon cinnamon*
- 1 *tablespoon ground ginger*

Place brown sugar, molasses and shortening in large saucepan. Cook over medium heat, stirring frequently, until well blended. Sift together flour, baking soda, cinnamon and ginger; stir into warm molasses mixture until well blended. While dough is still warm, remove about one quarter of the dough; knead in hands to shape into a fine-grained ball. Roll out on lightly floured surface to a rectangle about $\frac{1}{8}''$ thick and large enough to cut out pieces needed. Repeat with remaining dough until all pieces of the house are cut out. Place carefully on greased cookie sheet. Bake in a moderately hot oven (375°) until edges barely begin to brown and surface is no longer puffy, about 5 to 8 minutes. Remove carefully to racks; cool.

To make gingerbread house:
Cut out – as indicated in drawing – and bake:
2 pieces (3 × 7″) for walls. Cut out windows and door as indicated in drawing.
2 pieces (4 × 8″) for roof.
2 pieces (4 × 5″) for front and back. Cut out edges and window as indicated in drawing.
4 pieces (1 × 3″, 1 × 2″ and 2 pieces 1 × 3″) for chimney. Cut off edges as indicated in drawing.

Decorate sides and roof with frosting to outline windows, doors, roof tiles, window boxes etc.; let dry. Spread frosting on ends of sides and on roof pieces where they meet; assemble chimney. Put house together; place chimney on top. Let stand until firm.

Frosting:
- 1 *egg white*
- 2 *cups sifted confectioners' sugar*
- 1 *teaspoon lemon juice*

Place all ingredients in small deep mixing bowl. Beat at high speed until firm. It should be of a soft enough consistency to flow through a fine pastry tube to make the decorations, but stiff enough to hold its shape. While mixing, add a few drops more lemon juice or a tablespoon more or less of sugar, to obtain this consistency. Decorate Gingerbread House.

Gingerbread house – see recipe page 89

Kitchen terms

Aspic
A stiff gelatine obtained by combining fish or meat bouillon with gelatine powder.

Au gratin
Obtained by covering a dish with a white sauce (usually prepared with grated cheese) and then heating the dish in the oven so that a golden crust forms.

Baste
To moisten meat or other foods while cooking to add flavor and to prevent drying of the surface. The liquid is usually melted fat, meat drippings, fruit juice or sauce.

Blanch (precook)
To preheat in boiling water or steam. (1) Used to inactivate enzymes and shrink food for canning, freezing, and drying. Vegetables are blanched in boiling water or steam, and fruits in boiling fruit juice, sirup, water, or steam. (2) Used to aid in removal of skins from nuts, fruits, and some vegetables.

Blend
To mix thoroughly two or more ingredients.

Bouillon
Brown stock, conveniently made by dissolving a bouillon cube in water.

Broth
Water in which meat, fish or vegetables have been boiled or cooked.

'En papillote'
Meat, fish or vegetables wrapped in grease-proof paper or aluminum foil (usually first sprinkled with oil or butter, herbs and seasonings) and then baked in the oven or grilled over charcoal. Most of the taste and aroma are preserved in this way.

Fold
To combine by using two motions, cutting vertically through the mixture and turning over and over by sliding the implement across the bottom of the mixing bowl with each turn.

Fry
To cook in fat; applied especially (1) to cooking in a small amount of fat, also called sauté or pan-fry; (2) to cooking in a deep layer of fat, also called deep-fat frying.

Marinate
To let food stand in a marinade usually an oil–acid mixture like French dressing.

Parboil
To boil until partially cooked. The cooking is usually completed by another method.

Poach
To cook in a hot liquid using precautions to retain shape. The temperature used varies with the food.

Reduce
To concentrate the taste and aroma of a particular liquid or food e.g. wine, bouillon, soup, sauce etc. by boiling in a pan with the lid off so that the excess water can evaporate.

Roast
To cook, uncovered, by dry heat. Usually done in an oven, but occasionally in ashes, under coals or on heated stones or metals. The term is usually applied to meats but may refer to other food as potatoes, corn, chestnuts.

Sauté
To brown or cook in a small amount of fat. See Fry.

Simmer
To cook in a liquid just below the boiling point, at temperatures of 185°–210°. Bubbles form slowly and collapse below the surface.

Skim
To take away a layer of fat from soup, sauces, etc.

Stock
The liquid in which meat or fish has been boiled together with herbs and vegetables.

Whip
To beat rapidly to produce expansion, due to incorporation of air as applied to cream, eggs, and gelatin dishes.

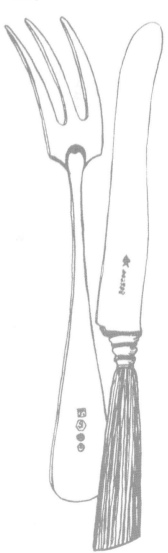

Conversion tables

Liquid measures

American
standard cup

metric equivalent
(approximately)

1 cup = $\frac{1}{2}$ pint   = 8 fl. oz. (fluid ounce) = 2,37 dl (deciliter)
1 tbs. (tablespoon) = $\frac{1}{2}$ fl. oz.   = 1,5 cl (centiliter)
1 tsp. (teaspoon)   = $\frac{1}{6}$ fl. oz.   = 0,5 cl
1 pint   = 16 fl. oz.   = 4,73 dl
1 quart = 2 pints = 32 fl. oz.   = 9,46 dl

British
standard cup

metric equivalent
(approximately)

1 cup = $\frac{1}{2}$ pint   = 10 fl. oz.   = 2,84 dl
1 tbs.   = 0.55 fl. oz.   = 1,7 cl
1 tsp.   = $\frac{1}{5}$ fl. oz.   = 0,6 cl
1 pint   = 20 fl. oz.   = 5,7 dl
1 quart = 2 pints = 40 fl. oz.   = 1,1 l (liter)

1 cup = 16 tablespoons
1 tablespoon = 3 teaspoons

1 liter = 10 deciliter = 100 centiliter

Oven temperatures

Centigrade	Fahrenheit	
up to 105° C	up to 225° F	cool
105–135° C	225–275° F	very slow
135–160° C	275–325° F	slow
175–190° C	350–375° F	moderate
215–230° C	400–450° F	hot
230–260° C	450–500° F	very hot
260° C	500° F	extremely hot

Solid measures

American/British

metric equivalent
(approximately)

1 lb. (pound)   = 16 oz. (ounces)   = 453 g (gram)
        1 oz.   = 28   g
2.2 lbs.   = 1000 g = 1 kg (kilogram)
        $3\frac{1}{2}$ oz.   = 100   g

46 Stuffed herring, Norwegian
49 Tuna fish casserole, Norwegian

Poultry and game dishes

52 Black pot, Norwegian
51 Chicken, Swedish
51 Fried chicken, Danish
52 Goose fat
52 Rabbit fricassee, Finnish
51 Roast chicken, Swedish
52 Samsoe chicken, Danish

Meat dishes

54 Baked ham and eggs, Danish
63 Beef à la Lindström, Swedish
58 Beef and ham birds, Danish
63 Boiled beef, Swedish
62 Cabbage pudding, Swedish
56 Collops, Swedish
62 Crown of lamb, Norwegian
59 Dill meat, Finnish
55 Frosted meat loaf, Swedish
62 Ground liver steak, Danish
54 Ham and potato dinner, Danish
53 Ham rolls, Swedish
56 Hash, Swedish
62 Kidney hash, Swedish
61 Lamb and cabbage stew, Norwegian

57 Lamb steaks, Finnish
60 Lamb stew, Finnish
58 Loin of pork, Danish
57 Loin of pork, Swedish
56 Meat balls, Danish
54 Meat balls, Swedish
55 Meat cakes garni, Swedish
55 Meat dumplings, Swedish
56 Pork chops, Swedish
57 Pot roast, Swedish
54 Roast fresh ham, Finnish
58 Roast fresh ham, Swedish
58 Roast pork, Swedish
63 Sailor's stew, Norwegian
59 Sausage casserole, Swedish
63 Steak and onions, Norwegian
59 Veal rollettes, Swedish
59 Veal timbale, Swedish

Desserts

67 Apple sauce, Danish
65 Baked apples with almond filling, Swedish
68 Baked pancake, Swedish
66 Berry cream, Swedish
67 Caramelcream, Norwegian
69 Caramel mold, Swedish
68 Cream waffles, Swedish
69 Crisp pancakes, Swedish
65 Custard, Swedish
64 Dried fruit cream, Swedish
68 Egg waffies, Swedish
66 Fruit jelly with cream, Norwegian
67 Lemon delight, Danish

69 Poor knights, Norwegian
66 Rhubarb cream, Swedish
68 Rice fritters, Finnish
67 Rice porridge, Norwegian
69 Veiled country lass, Danish
66 Whipped farina, Swedish

Cakes and Pastries

70 Almond filled buns, Danish
71 Apple cake, Danish
70 Bread and almond filled buns, Danish
73 Brown spice cookies, Swedish
72 Caramel-iced cake, Finnish
71 Cheese cake, Swedish
72 Chiffon cake, Norwegian
76 Country lasses, Swedish
73 Cream cake, Swedish
71 Crown cake, Swedish
73 Light sponge cake, Finnish
76 Lucia gingersnaps, Swedish
72 Marstrand cookies, Danish
71 Marzipan cakes, Danish
74 Pastries, Danish
70 Plain buns, Swedish
70 Shortbread, Finnish

Beverages

77 Eggcream, Norwegian
77 Fruit juice glogg, Swedish
77 Glogg, Swedish
77 Mumma, Swedish

77 Wine cooler, Danish

Traditional Christmas dishes

83 Baked ham with mustard sauce, Danish
82 Boiled pig's feet, Swedish
81 Braised red cabbage, Norwegian
87 Chocolate ice, Finnish
87 Chocolate toffee, Finnish
82 Christmas ham, Swedish
85 Christmas punch, Swedish
80 Delicatessen meatballs, Swedish
88 Gingerbread house
82 Ham, Finnish
79 Herring salad, Danish
80 Jellied veal, Swedish
79 Liver paté, Swedish
79 Liver paté in aspic, Swedish
85 Peter Heering delight, Danish
81 Red cabbage, Norwegian
85 Rice pudding, Danish
80 Roast goose, Swedish
81 Sweetened potato pudding, Finnish
85 Tijinuski caramels, Finnish
87 Toffee, Swedish
81 Turnip pie, Finnish